7.9.82

For Eric my friend
and more luff too—
since we've both
tried to climb the
writers mountian
he knows the
meaning of Weiji *

Carroll 2

* 27 page

THE PEAK
EXPERIENCE

THE PEAK EXPERIENCE

Hiking and Climbing for Women

Carroll Seghers II

The Bobbs-Merrill Company, Inc.
Indianapolis / New York

Excerpt by Molly Higgins pp. ix-x reprinted from *Climb: Rock Climbing in Colorado* by Bob Godfrey and Dudley Chelton by permission of Alpine House. Copyright 1977.

The lines from "The First Elegy" of *Duino Elegies* by Rainer Maria Rilke, translated by J. B. Leishman and Stephen Spender, are reprinted with the permission of W. W. Norton & Company, Inc. Copyright 1939 by W. W. Norton & Company, Inc. Copyright renewed 1967 by Stephen Spender and J. B. Leishman.

Excerpt from *Climbing Blind* by Colette Richard, translated by Norman Dale. Copyright © 1966 by Hodder & Stoughton Ltd., London, and E. P. Dutton, Inc. By permission of E. P. Dutton.

Excerpt from Arlene Blum's diary printed with the permission of Arlene Blum.

Wind chill table reprinted with the permission of the United States Department of Commerce, National Oceanic and Atmospheric Administration.

The excerpts from *The Wilderness Handbook* by Paul Petzoldt are reprinted with the permission of W. W. Norton & Company, Inc. Copyright 1974 by Paul Petzoldt.

Published by The Bobbs-Merrill Company, Inc.
Indianapolis   New York
Designed by Rita Muncie
Manufactured in the United States of America
First printing

Library of Congress Cataloging in Publication Data

Seghers, Carroll, II, 1924–

The peak experience.

Bibliography: p.
Includes index.
1. Mountaineering. 2. Sports for women.
I. Title.
GV200.S43   796.5'22   78-11205
ISBN 0-672-52487-2
ISBN 0-672-52488-0 pbk.

This book is dedicated to Paul Petzoldt,
that grand old mountaineer of the West,
because he started so many, my daughters included,
toward "the joy of wilderness";
and to Lynne Spaulding, my editor,
who started me up the writer's mountain.

Acknowledgments

To: Heidi DeLay, who did the very nearly perfect line drawings in the book, which thrilled me almost as much as her "first time ever" climbing for the pictures in the chapter "On the Wall—One Woman's First Climb." Her talent and true grit were exciting to see.

Special thanks for research and typing to Nancy Okie, who somehow interpreted this author's clumsy handwriting.

For the fine photographs of exotic peaks on page 41, thanks to Jack Miller for the one of Bolivia and to John Cleare for that of the Himalayas.

My greatest debt is to those women climbers I've been privileged to know, to know about, or to climb with. Each has conveyed to me in a very personal way her experience of the "highs" that I want you to know too. Those women are Molly Higgins, Irene Miller, Beverly Johnson, Arlene Blum, Barbara Eastman, Monica Jackson, Beata Sauerlander, Mona Levine, Krystyna Palmoroska, Joan Moffet Hemingway, Calla Corner, Jennifer Langdon, Sue Engles, Betty Seghers, Loraine Seghers, Diane Shoutis, Amy Phillips, Lauria Low, Sue Swedlund, Irene Ortenberger, Nea Morin, Micheline Morin, Wanda Rutkiewicz, Junko Tabei, Colette Richards, Sara Jane Bates, Anne Cannon, Mary Lou Fox, Leslie Freeman, Carol Genebach, Mary Jo Hudson, Beverly B. May, Jeanne Ross, Carole Strickler, and Valerie Turtle.

And finally, a thanks to Denise Marcil, my literary agent, who took my film treatment for an all-woman climb and turned it into a book. Without her we would not be meeting here!

CONTENTS

GETTING UP

"My boy friend is spending the week with another girl, my employer told me he'd rather hire men, I feel as if I've been arguing for weeks, and I'm sick of it!" I said, stomping over to the door of my cabin and looking out into Eldorado Canyon. The spring day was an interlude between storms, and Redgarden Wall beckoned warmly.

Charlotte said, "You've been wanting to lead Green Spur; let's go do it."

I'd never led 5.9 and Charlotte had never followed it. Our dubious glances met and we laughed nervously as I thought, "A climb like that should let me forget my troubles."

As we hiked around the west side of Redgarden Wall, its massive buttresses and towers caught the afternoon sun. Stumbling up the scree, I kept my eyes at my feet until Charlotte exclaimed, "Look at the way the green and yellow lichens streak across the rock bands!" I looked up, wondering at the color of the rock, at the pigeons soaring above, then at the pleasure of being out with a good friend.

When the climb came into view, we noticed another party using the fixed pitons to climb the second pitch. "If it's that hard, will I be able to do it?"

Charlotte smiled and patted my back.

At the first belay stance, we contemplated the pitch stretching above, the crux. A corner and a jam crack ran parallel for one hundred feet; then they merged into a thirty-foot dihedral that was steep and smooth. As I tightened my shoes, Charlotte said, "I feel like your sister at your piano recital."

The move off the ledge was tricky. "I'm gymnasting all around here, and I can't seem to figure it out," I told Charlotte as a layback worked through to a jam. Climbing the parallel dihedral and jam crack grew progressively more difficult. With my feet sometimes in the crack, sometimes on the face, my balance was always changing; I worked back and forth between the two cracks like a dancer using the whole stage.

At the base of the dihedral, I found a face of minute holds. With no more secure jams, it required a change in dynamics like the Surprise Symphony. *I moved up, thinking only of the small holds, of placing my feet precisely, of not shaking. The combination of control and anxiety enveloped me completely until I traversed right, deliberately, carefully, out onto larger holds. I flashed Charlotte an "OK," laughed joyously, and clambered to the belay ledge.*

Charlotte followed. She looked like a spring nymph, with her dark hair in braids, her rosy cheeks, and an ever-growing grin as she figured out the moves. "You're doing it, Charlotte!" I yelled.

When she pulled up onto the belay stance, we hugged each other, then prepared to rappel off. I said, "I loved the intensity of those hard moves. I loved the complete immersion of myself. Did I take too long? Did you get bored?"

Charlotte smiled and answered, "It doesn't matter. I enjoy the sunshine, enjoy being up here; I love being as high as the birds!"

—Molly Higgins

FOREWORD

I have always desired to be good at some physical activity. I wanted to see just how far I could go if I took something seriously and focused my attention on it. I always admired my male and female peers who could outrun, outthrow and outswim me, for as a kid I was squat and chubby. When I was asked to describe my abilities in sports, "uncoordinated" was the first word that came to my mind.

So it was with some astonishment that I discovered I had some aptitude for climbing. When I was eighteen I joined the college club and was thoroughly mesmerized by ropes, carabiners, down jackets, and a spirit of adventure and love for the Rocky Mountains. I enrolled in all of the club's classes on rock climbing, and I rarely missed a peak climb or an overnight. Since it has always been one of my cardinal rules to avoid misery whenever possible, I took up jogging, figuring that if I was fit I could avoid the breathless, sweating, expiring feelings that can make an outing seem like the end of the world. Later I lifted a few weights. (Actually I only used the weight bar with the weights stripped off, but it all helped make hiking and climbing easier.)

In the early seventies I committed myself to climbing as well as I could. I searched out areas renowned for the great variety of their routes—Eldorado Canyon, Yosemite Valley, Rocky Mountain National Park, and Canada—areas in which I could hone my skills and delight in the different mountain ecosystems. Consequently, I met many fine women climbers: Bev Johnson, Arlene Blum, Diana Hunter. They were inspiring role models for me, almost heroines, who indicated that I too might climb high peaks and steep rock walls.

During this time I also met Barb Eastman, who liked to drink tea and climb rocks as much as I did. We were at about the same ability level: pretty good but nothing to marvel at. We both climbed conservatively—safety mattered most. For four years we spent a month together each spring and fall. In Yosemite Valley we coached each other up many intimidating climbs; we shared dreams of climbing the big walls together; and we chatted happily about the lichens, the canyon wrens, and our sore hands. Supportiveness was the rule. We became good buddies and then deeply committed friends. I'll never forget one late afternoon in particular when Barb cleaned my glasses as I whimpered on her shoulder because I was so tired from the thousand feet of climbing below us. Comforted, I gathered my strength and led on to the top of the buttress. Since nightfall was imminent and the descent was clifted and unknown to us, we curled up beside a little fire and tried to forget how thirsty and tired we were until morning.

My climbing experiences have been some of the richest moments of my life. I have had to rely on other people and on myself to an extent that I might

not otherwise have experienced. I have been intimately exposed to places—from the red sandstone
cliffs of Utah to the snowy ridges of the Pamir Mountains. The most exciting fact is that these experiences
are accessible to any woman of any age who has a taste
for beauty and adventure. The mountainous world is
so varied that its rewards are available to both the
mellow and the daring.

Carroll Seghers's book *The Peak Experience* is an exciting introduction for anyone who wishes either to
begin hiking and climbing or just to learn more about
it. He tackles the subject with a probing thoroughness
that may be all the more enlightening because of his
male objectivity. He explores the motivations for
climbing with such sensitivity that anyone can gain an
appreciation of why women climb. He solicits many
points of view—from college women, from a blind
woman, from a housewife, and from women who are
totally dedicated to climbing. He describes some very
impressive female ascents, from those by Victorian
ladies who grappled with their skirts to Vera Komarkova's and Irene Miller's recent ascent of Annapurna I.

Carroll gives good concrete advice, especially on
getting in shape and on selecting boots. He discusses
food selection, clothing, and general trip preparation
with the touch of a perfectionist. He also covers the
gray areas of a wilderness trip by describing the degrees of conscientiousness and consideration that will
make anyone a better woodsperson. He encourages a
leadership role for women, or at least a position of
mutual responsibility. This is important, for, one
grows most from the experience by assuming
responsibility.

The rewards of the mountains are abundant, and

Carroll Seghers's book will help anyone plan that first trip. After that, it's up to the individual to go! Get out the door and feel some of the most incredible joys and see some of the incredible places of this world.

—Molly Higgins

Molly Higgins and Barb Eastman on El Capitan.

THE PEAK
EXPERIENCE

1 | INTRODUCTION

And what joy, think ye, did they feel after the exceeding long and troublous ascent? —after scrambling, slipping, pulling, pushing, lifting, gasping, looking, hoping, despairing, climbing, holding on, falling off, trying, puffing, loosing, gathering, talking, stepping, grumbling, anathematizing, scraping, hacking, bumping, jogging, overturning, hunting, straddling—for know ye that by these methods alone are the most divine mysteries of the Quest revealed?

—Professor Norman Collie
From the *Scottish Mountaineering Journal*, 1894

To that list, female climbers have been adding *sighing* and *smiling*! As a human endeavor, climbing must be as old as hunting, and none of the action from those times has changed. What has changed are the terrain, the elevations, the equipment, and the varied forms of the "Quest."

In the period between 1854 and 1865, when most of the Alpine peaks were first scaled, the methods and the tools were as basic as the early hunters' spears and arrows: hobnailed boots and climbing irons, crude ice axes and Manila rope. In the Golden Age, those early ascents were simple basic expedition climbs, usually made in the best summer months, with the climbers

1

leaving from a nearby hotel with guides and supplies
for a few days at most. These early feats were re-
markable for their daring of the unknown. A thrill,
something akin to the experience of the caveman who
killed the first tiger with only a spear. "Conquering"
was the emotional feeling of early climbers and a
word much used in their writings.

It should come as quite a surprise that in that Victorian era the ladies were formidable "peak baggers."
Men wrote and published their own books in those
days of classic male chauvinism, but it was not in masculine fashion to write about the ladies. Besides, for a
Christian minister (many of whom, too, were climbing
enthusiasts) to talk of female athletes might seem las-
civious, even if those ladies were trying to get closer to
God—unless one was his aunt, and he was the editor
of an alpine journal. I began this book with the mis-
taken impression that women were only now ventur-
ing up mountains in the spirit of a new freedom
(Women's Lib) and eco-consciousness. I assumed that
these modern women of the 1960s and -70s were the
avant-garde of women climbers, until I discovered
that detailed records of the following little-known Ms.
history survive today, thanks to one minister's and the
Swiss guides' archival bent plus rare books. Those
female climbers truly astonish me.

The earliest woman climber recorded was Miss
Parminter, who climbed on Le Buet in the Savoie
Alps in 1799. (A year later this mountain became the
scene of the first recorded death of a climber in a
crevasse—a male, of course. Nowhere is it recorded
that a woman died of a climbing accident in those
years.)

Other "firsts" followed: in 1808, Marie Paradis, a

maidservant, became the first woman to climb Mont
Blanc. Two Scottish ladies, Mrs. and Miss Campbell,
made a successful crossing of the Col du Géant from
Chamonix to Courmayeur (11,000 feet) between
France and Italy in the Mont Blanc massif in 1822.

Two other extraordinary women climbers of the
Golden Age were Miss Meta Brevoort, an American,
and Miss Lucy Walker. Their records are phenom-
enal. Lucy Walker, born into a family of climbers
from Liverpool, made ninety-eight expeditions over a
period of twenty years. With her father and her
brother, she made the first major ascents by a woman.
In 1865 she made the second crossing of the Moming
Pass at 12,444 feet, and six years later the fourth ascent of the Eiger. In 1871 she became the first woman
to reach the top of the Matterhorn. It is said of Miss
Walker that she invariably wore women's clothing for
climbing and lived on a diet of sponge cake, cham-
pagne and Asti Spumante while on an expedition.

Miss Brevoort was the aunt of Reverend William
Augustus Brevoort Coolidge, with whom she made
many climbs until her death in 1876. Their dog,
Tschingel, often accompanied them. It is reported
that Miss Brevoort sometimes wore trousers in des-
peration, the skirt being one of many great impedi-
ments to Victorian lady climbers.

"Small rings should be sewn inside the seam of the
dress," one notable woman mountain traveler of the
1850s, a Miss Cole, advised, "and a cord passed
through them, the ends of which should be knotted
together in such a way that the whole dress may be
drawn up the required height at a moment's notice. A
riding skirt, without a body, which can be slipped off
and on in a moment, is also invaluable." At which Miss

Brevoort complained, "Even so, snow enters the rings and stuffs up the hem and makes me heavy and wet. I have had to baste up both dress and skirt."

Tschingel and her owners' climbing feats are so numerous that a summary would read like *The Guinness Book of Records*. In eleven years the dog climbed thirty peaks and crossed thirty-six passes. Their story exists because Coolidge was editor of the *Alpine Journal* from 1880 to 1889.

Another great woman climber was Miss Isabella Straton, who had an income of £4,000 a year. She started at the age of twenty-three in 1861 in the Mont Blanc range, and ten years later made the first ascent of the Aiguille de Moine between the Mer de Glace and the Glacier de Talèfre; she climbed the Punta Isabella, named after her, in 1875, and the Aiguille de la Persévérance the same year. She made the first winter ascent of Mont Blanc with Jean Charlet, a Chamonix guide with whom she climbed from 1865 and later married.

The amazing adventures of Miss Annie Peck stretch the imagination to the limit. An American schoolmistress, she did not even begin her mountaineering career until she was forty-seven, when she tackled the Matterhorn. In 1908, when she was fifty-eight, on a second attempt in withering cold weather, she reached the unclimbed 21,134-foot north summit of Huascarán in the Cordillera Blanca of Peru, the highest known peak in that day: a truly Herculean first ascent, accompanied only by two Swiss guides from Zermatt, neither of whom had ever climbed outside the Swiss Alps. Annie had to engineer and finance the entire project.

For sheer extravagant outrageous courage, treasure

Opposite: Annie Peck, *ca.* 1900.

up Gertrude Bell, a friend of T. E. Lawrence. An explorer-archaeologist to boot, she made a protracted attack with a group on the unclimbed northeast face of the Finsteraarhorn in Bernese Oberland, spending forty-eight hours roped on it, caught immobilized by a blizzard. Of Miss Bell, a woman of average size, a visiting Arab chief is said to have remarked, ". . . and this is one of their women! Allah, what must their men be like?"

Miriam O'Brien Underhill, New England–born, who had taken part in expeditions—all led by men—on the major European peaks, introduced in the 1920s what she quaintly called "manless climbing," and went on to a list of spectacular firsts.

The Swiss had their own great female climbers. One, "Loulou Boulaz," who began in the 1930s, made a first ascent of the north face of the Zinal Rothorn, a third ascent of Mont Blanc by the Pear route, a third ascent of the Grandes Jorasses by the Central Spur, a second ascent of the north face of the Petit Dru and the north face of the Aiguille Verte. Together with Lulu Durand, she made some outstanding first feminine climbs in the Chamonix district: on the Reguin, a traverse of the Grand Charmoz from left to right by the southwest face and northwest ridge, and the southwest face of the Dent du Géant. In 1937 she made one of the first attempts on the north face of the Eiger. Later, she climbed the north face of the Grandes Jorasses by the Walker Spur, and with Pierre Bounant she made the first feminine ascent of the Furggen ridge of the Matterhorn.

And in 1946 there was Nea Morin and Micheline Morin, sisters-in-law, who made the first *cordée feminine* (woman's climb) of the Chapeau, a corner of the Reguin, and the southwest ridge of Aiguille de Moine. In 1953 Nea and Denise (a daughter) made the first traverse of three peaks of the Dolomites— the Winkler, the Stakeler, and the Delago. Then they did the first *cordée feminine* on the north face of Cima Piccola di Cavaredo, and with Nea leading, daughter and E. H. Marriott following, they traversed the north ridge of the Weissmies. Nea also made record ascents of the Matterhorn.

For nearly two centuries "petticoats" had been attacking their mountaintops, but it was not until 1978 that the Swiss Alpine Club accepted its first female member; that is, 179 years after Miss Parminter! The Alpine Club of London, probably the oldest climbing society in continual existence, did not accept women either, until it merged with the seventy-two-year-old Ladies' Alpine Club in 1976.

On summit expeditions, the eighteenth-century lady climbers had to surmount near-vertical rock and ice and all manner of snow conditions with simple tools, flawed techniques, the worst garments, and no press recognition. Today's women are climbing all over the world, and not without media fanfare. Women of several nations have made record ascents. In 1975 Wanda Rutkiewicz led a group of men and women up what was then the highest unclimbed peak in the world, Gasherbrum 2 in Pakistan. Two Polish women roped together and alone made it to the top. And an all-woman Polish team climbed the same mountain that year.

On May 16, 1975, an all-woman Japanese team put the first female on top of Mount Everest. She was Junko Tabei—thirty-five years old, five feet tall, weighing ninety-two pounds, the mother of a three-year-old daughter—who had trained three years and had given piano lessons in Saitama, her home, to raise the $5,000 she needed to join the expedition as Deputy Leader. On May 18, 1975, the Chinese press reported that a woman in a group of Tibetan climbers reached the top of Mount Everest from another side.

Why do they do it? I've asked that question of women climbers the world over for the last ten years. I ask, not because I think it strange that the "gentle" sex should seek what is traditionally thought to be a "macho" type activity, but because I am truly in awe of the skill and enthusiasm exhibited. In fact, I ask the question because women's traditional role would certainly excuse them from any such hardship competition. Yet they seek it and thrive. Why?

The answer: in great part, for all the usual reasons that men are drawn to the wilderness and mountain climbing. A young college girl told me, "There are many interrelated reasons for my climbing. The terrible pure beauty of the mountains in winter, the comradeship, the confrontation of fear, the intensity of the experience in and of itself, the freedom from constraint, the redeeming necessity of every action, the absolute commitment."

I am convinced that, as a group, women respond more to the aesthetic experience of nature. It's not so much the challenge, as it is with men, who seek to make "first ascents" or to climb the hardest routes. Women are sensitive to the subtle beauties of nature, the majesty of the mountains, the ultimate communion. Living in the rawest elements touches their souls in a way few men know. Women do identify with mother earth. In a very real sense it is this quality that gives them the edge over men as climbers for certain expeditions. The feeling of competing with their climbing partners which men suffer does not usually affect the female climber, who shares wholeheartedly in any chore that benefits the group. She saves herself the stress of comparisons. She's glad to be there and is not "keeping score."

It's not just the record assaults that have lured modern women; it's the beauty, the escape, the freedom in nature, a simpler society than the pressure of metropolitan life. In America, women's sports are booming—a reaction to a new self-realization for which hiking and climbing have become the perfect expression. Women who hike and climb are fit, but youth and physical strength are not prerequisites to the enjoyment of the wilderness experience. The variety of hiking and climbing adventures for women is unlimited, from trail hiking to scaling the Himalayas. There is no climbing season.

In January of 1974 I spent two weeks, sometimes at forty below, with a coed group climbing the Grand Teton. Not all of us made the summit that time, but Helen Higbee of Lander, Wyoming, age thirty, became the first woman to reach the peak in winter.

It took us ten days of skiing uphill and two days of climbing to reach the famous hut on the saddle that would be base camp for our peak attempt. The hut was like a corrugated freezer. We of the second assault crowded in to escape the sixty-mile-an-hour gusts. These gusts, combined with an outside temperature of thirty below, made the dark interior seem downright cozy, with candle glow and steam from our cook pots. It was in this atmosphere that I later watched the rapt, spellbound expression on the face

of Dave Greenberg of Great Neck, New York, age
nineteen, as he joined the circle of our bodies warming the inside of the stunted metal shell. He had just
spent twelve hours constantly exposed, struggling to
reach the Teton peak by 1:00 P.M. and then get back
to the hut before dark. His party had fallen short of
reaching the peak by a mere 150 feet. Time had run
out on them before they had reached the top. Nevertheless, his face, framed by a thick mop of dark curls,
shone like a saint's in the candlelight; his expression
was no less than beatific. He had the serenity of one
who had cast his eyes on the Creator and come away
with a vision. He was bombarded with questions from
all sides. With a half-smile he gazed through shiny
brown eyes at each questioner, as though there were
no oral language and eyes alone could talk. The fact is
that he was virtually in a state of shock; he'd been
hanging onto footholds, ropes, crevices, companions,
and his own nerves for such a long day—it had begun
and ended in the dark—that this community of
people was like rain to parched earth. He was soaking
it up in helpless silence. Later, he told me how "scary"
it was. His reason for the climb, he said, was to prove
himself by accepting some super challenge. He had
taken other NOLS (National Outdoor Leadership
School) summer trips and had found the outdoor life
quite gratifying, especially for a city boy. "To climb
the Teton in winter had to be the ultimate." Would he
ever do it again? His answer, "Never." The fright of
hanging out over the "belly roll"—a name for a narrow crawl space—even though roped, "blew my
mind." I asked him again as we waited at the airport
days later. His answer was the same. "I'll never try a
dangerous climb again; it was too hairy." He had no
regrets, but this Teton climb had done it for him. No

doubt he would find it easy to settle into his next semester at Reed College.

Lauria Low of Boulder, Colorado, twenty-four, had been with Dave that day. She had climbed the north face of the Teton with a top climber the summer before. Her reaction to and reasons for this winter climb were very different from Dave's. But in the hut that night her baby-blue eyes were glowing, and her every movement revealed an electric excitement from the day's happenings. Lauria told me that these summit climbs gave her the greatest five minutes of joyous peak feelings she'd ever known in her life. "A feeling of transcending to a new being, surpassing by the effort the person I was before. Moving to a new level, a permanent step up!" Her depth of sensitivity was stimulating. This college senior revealed to me more about man's fascination for mountains in ten minutes than a shelf full of published authorities. She told me that she habitually experienced great fears and anxieties in her everyday life. The confrontation with the real fears of climbing and the triumphs over these fears were her inspiration. A poem she carried expressed her discovery:

> *Who, if I cried, would hear me among the angelic*
> *orders? And even if one of them suddenly*
> *pressed me against his heart I should fade in*
> *   the strength of his*
> *stronger existence. For Beauty's nothing*
> *but beginning of Terror we're still just able to bear,*
> *and why we adore it so is because it serenely*
> *disdains to destroy us. Each single angel is terrible.*
> *And so I keep down my heart, and swallow the call-note*
> *of depth-dark sobbing.*
>
> —Rainer Maria Rilke
> *Duino Elegies*

On a six-week expedition in the Wind River Mountains of Wyoming, I've hiked and climbed with a mixed group that included women of all ages and backgrounds. With one wife, I've climbed in the Swiss and Italian Alps, and with another, the major walls in the East and in Yosemite. I have talked with or climbed with dozens of other climbers. These and other women, listed in my Acknowledgments, are or were super hikers and climbers. All found the "mountain highs" (a healthy altered state of consciousness) from climbing to have lasting rewards.

The desire to have peak experiences, to transcend the limitations of ordinary consciousness, operates in all of us. It is so basic that it seems like an inborn drive. Almost as soon as infants learn to sit up, they begin to rock themselves into highs. Later, as young children they learn to whirl into other states of awareness or to hyperventilate out of ordinary reality.

What makes mountaineering a means to alter consciousness in a combination of factors. First, there are the surroundings. The natural elevation of mountain summits over the surrounding land affords the climber magnificent vistas, as well as a bird's-eye view of environmental perspectives. When you are climbing high, the composition of the air you are breathing is changing. The higher above sea level you are, the lower the oxygen content of the air. The effort to climb most mountains will change your breathing pattern and your heartbeat. These in turn will change the amount of oxygen in the blood reaching your brain and will help produce a "high." Another factor affecting mountain climbers is the negatively ionized air high above sea level. Most urban environments abound in positively ionized air. By contrast, negative ions give feelings of alertness and mild excitation.

When you climb a mountain, you are facing a challenge. Successful completion of the challenge, endurance of the hardships along the way, and the exercise of your skills can provide unique satisfaction. I believe the act of mountain climbing gives one the most complete feeling of aliveness possible. Everything you are—every instinct, every skill, strength, power, intelligence, self-knowledge—is focused and narrowly concentrated on a single goal that allows no instant of deviation from the objective.

Achieving the summit, then descending, produces an aura of incredible exuberance; the feeling that one has wings all over one's body. "The euphoria that comes with high-risk exercise is pure, unencumbered by any degree of doubt or fear. It is deep, mellow, comforting, free," according to Dr. S. R. Rosenthal. "This source of joy from risk exercise is in the culture of man."

Peak experiences are those highlights of our lives that give us awareness and insight into a deeper level of existence. It is these events that change our way of viewing reality. Edward Rosenfeld, in *The Book of Highs,* characterizes a peak experience as the spontaneous awareness of twelve separate points, every one of which can be recognized as an element of climbing:

Detachment and objectivity	Unity
Ends rather than means	Nonjudgment
Time/space disorientation	Ego-transcendence
Transcendence of dichotomies	Self-trust
Strong sense of "free will"	Receptivity
Humility and surrender	Strong self-identity

To understand the feelings of women in the mountain realm, read Colette Richards's book *Climbing*

Blind. Without sight since the age of two and able only to tell night from day, this Frenchwoman reached the summit of Mont Blanc du Tacal (over 13,000 feet) and other peaks in the Chamonix massif between 1960 and 1962.

. . . I have always had an intense longing for space and great expeditions. I believe strongly in the truth of my inward feelings, and it is the idea I have of things which gives so much value to my mountains.

People are often surprised by my evocation of the mountains and my love of them. But sight is only one of our senses. There are all the things one perceives by other means, things one knows by intuition, things one can hear and touch and smell and taste. In foothills there are waterfalls, flowers, cattle bells and raspberries. What one experiences at higher altitudes is to my mind more precious and rare because it is difficult of access. The wind in the peaks, the footsteps of the rope party in the snow, the steady crunch of the ice axe sinking into it, the falling stones which whistle as they fall, avalanches, the sounds coming from the glaciers' depth. And there is also, which is wonderful to me, the reflection of brilliant sunshine on untrodden snow, the warmth, the quiet, the extraordinary light that is to be found nowhere else. There is the keen, cold air that stings the cheeks, the delicate, almost inperceptible scent of snow which has in it something of pine, of grass and of flowers. There is the use we who are sightless must make of our hands, the feeling of rock and snow.

Why do I climb mountains? Quite simply because the mountains and I had to meet. I go for my pleasure and to conquer myself. I know of nothing more deadly than inaction—whether physical or mental. One needs to try one's strength and one's willpower to triumph over one's destiny, to remake oneself, to put one's muscles to use. . . . I do it because I love the beauty and simplicity of a way of living which

brings confidence, which confirms resolution ... calls for
courage.

But what of the dangers? Of course there have
been tragedies. Grace Holman, leader of the first all-
female ascent of Mount McKinley in Alaska in 1970,
lost her husband in a climbing accident in 1969; she
herself died while skiing on an Alaskan glacier in
1971. Irene Miller, who has participated in many
technical all-woman ascents, witnessed the freezing
death of another woman climber in Yosemite. In the
summer of 1974, nine Russian women died while
climbing Lenin Peak. Arlene Blum, an experienced
American climber who had also been attempting to
reach Lenin's summit that summer and who tried to
save her climbing companions from the same storm
that killed the Russians, says, "It's hard to refute the
notion that women climbers tend to press on impru-
dently to prove their abilities if you look at the Lenin
climb alone." From her diary:

> *Farther down we find Heide, Eva and Anya, a German*
> *climber, huddled in the snow, with the storm raging around*
> *them. "We are bivouacking here," Eva says, "Stay with us.*
> *We can surely reach the summit tomorrow."*
> *In my faltering German I say, "I am through with Peak*
> *Lenin. I am going down. Come with me. It is too dangerous*
> *to stay here without tents or stoves."*
> *"No. We will be safe here. Stay." I try to convince them to*
> *leave, but my struggle alone in the storm has left me too tired*
> *to argue anything with anybody, especially in German.*
> *I stumble down ... the wind blows me off my feet. I sit*
> *there. Finally I get up. Are we really going the right way?*
> *The snow is up to my face. I am so tired. We seem to have*
> *been fighting our way down for an eternity.*

We stumble into a break in the ridge. It's the break that leads to high camp. As we step down into the sheltered camp, there's sudden silence and relief from the storm.

I collapse outside the tent, too tired to take off my crampons. There are seven others somewhere above us on the summit ridge, exposed to the full fury of the storm, without tents or stoves or sleeping bags. I pray that they are all right.

Only six climbers came down to camp the morning after our summit attempt. Eva died of exposure on the summit ridge. So senseless. If only I had tried harder to persuade her to come down with me. If only things had been different.

Earlier, Arlene did climb with the first successful all-woman expedition to the summit of Mount McKinley in Alaska—21,300 feet. In October 1978 she led the first successful all-woman climb of the Himalayan peak Annapurna (26,504 feet). Irene Miller and Vera Komarkova reached the summit— the fourth expedition to reach it ever. Two others lost their lives. Said Blum, "I had known before that women could climb big mountains, and this expedition confirmed that. We're all still close friends. That doesn't always happen on an expedition."

American women climbers seem as intrepid as their western pioneer forebears. In the U.S., women's "manless climbing" began unheralded with a passion in recent times. Masters of rock climbing, Sue Swedlund and Irene Ortenberger climbed the north face of the Grand Teton in 1965. Sybille Hechtel and Beverly Johnson were the first women to climb El Capitan—over 3,000 feet—in 1973. In 1978, at age thirty-three, Johnson became the first woman to solo that wall.

New snow was falling, adding to the six inches of fine powder on all the roads in Boulder, when I finally trudged up to 623 Cascade Avenue. Sitting half inside, one leg outside, exposed to the fast-melting flakes; screwdriver in hand, working the crusted ice out of the aluminum track of a stuck sliding glass door, was Molly Higgins, mumbling something about architects' stupid Florida designs that don't work in Colorado Decembers. Molly flash-glanced me with slate-blue eyes behind granny glasses, long brown hair whipping while she kept chipping away at the ice that was blocking the door and letting in the night cold. She had the short, strong coupling of limbs that reminded me of the spring steel so well disguised in the round shape of ponies. Strong-handed and strong-minded, too. For the next two hours, between her packing for a skiing trip the next day and guests arriving and departing, I got to know and admire this twenty-eight-year-old "Ms. Climber" who has had such exciting times on the way up and down the many mountains in her life.

In 1974 Molly was the first American to scale Russia's Peak Lenin—23,405 feet—located in the Russian Pamir range in the Tadzhikistan Republic just north of Sinkiang Province, China. Her climb was achieved during a period of the most treacherous weather recorded in twenty-five years. One storm that summer took the lives of eight experienced Russian female alpine climbers and an American man, John Gray Ullin from Seattle. During that period Molly met another American woman, Arlene Blum, who failed to reach the summit but lived. In Russia that summer Molly ice-climbed a 2,000-foot face on a 15,000-foot peak with an English partner, male, and also survived an earthquake-triggered avalanche that crashed down to their mountain base, leaving fifty feet of debris. On short warning, she and other team members ducked into a crevasse as tons of snow thundered over them.

Molly started climbing in 1968 at eighteen with a boy friend at Colorado College, where she majored in biology. Her first rock climbing was done in the Garden of the Gods; then in 1971 at Colorado Outward Bound, where she later served as an instructor for several years. In between, she began honing her winter skills by climbing peaks in the San Juan Mountains. She did the first ladies' ascent of the Diamond on Longs Peak in Colorado with two other women, Stephanie Atwood and Lauri Manson. With Barbara Eastman, she climbed El Capitan in the spring of 1977, which was only the second time it had been scaled by an all-woman team and the first time by the "nose route." Molly trained for two years to spend three nights and four days scaling three grade-V faces in Yosemite Valley and one grade-VI face on El Capitan.

Today, she works in the laboratory of Boulder Community Hospital, training or climbing every day.

In the summer of 1976 I met two girls on top of Colorado's Arapo Pass at 12,200 feet who had been there two weeks on a near-starvation diet, sharing with four others three tins of sardines, a quarter pound of cheese and some tea. Each had a personal goal. Jennifer Langdon, twenty-two, a psychology major at Temple University, wanted to observe the human relationship under the greatest pressure— near starvation—for a college paper. Sue Engles, twenty-nine, an ex-PAA stewardess and climbing hobbyist, wanted even more. She was searching for the route to a new level of consciousness by experiencing starvation in a raw environment at high altitude.

Jennifer stayed twenty days, Sue twenty-two. After her reentry, Sue talked with me quite frankly about her experiences, mental and physical. When we said our goodbyes, her eyes searched mine for sincerity. Satisfied, trusting, she took a weathered card from her bag. Printed in a small feminine hand was a quotation from Aleister Crowley:

> *I meant to tell mankind to aspire to a new state about which I could tell them little or nothing, to teach them to tread a long and lonely path which might or might not lead thither, to bid them dare to encounter all possible perils of nature unknown, to abandon all their settled manners of living and to cut themselves off from their past and their environment, and to attempt a quixotic adventure with no resources beyond their native strength and sagacity. I had done it myself and found not only that the pearl of great price was worth far more than I possessed, but that the very perils and privations of the quest were themselves my dearest memories. I was certain of this, at least, that nothing in the world except this was worth doing.*

Women have one great physical advantage that fits them for hardship climbs. They generally resist the effects of cold temperatures better than the male. I say this for good biological reasons. A woman seems to know her body very well. She is more attuned to the changes and discomfort that occur from muscle strain or temperature variations. True, this means a lower pain threshold. In climbing, that's not a bad thing. "An early warning system" is more valuable than a "football player's sheer insensitivity to injury." *Hypothermia, Killer of the Unprepared*, by T. G. Lathrop, reveals the insidious nature of exposure for those who are not alert.

On the level of pure survival in hardship, wilderness experiences, woman's historical record in the pioneer age is amazing. Of the Donner Party in 1846, seventeen of eighty-seven (five women and twelve men) were lost for thirty-three days in a blinding snowstorm. The women proved to be hardier than the men: all five of the women who started out made it; only two of the men survived. The women survived, some by eating their own dead. A rescue party found Mrs. Jacob Donner and her children. The woman was nearly dead from starvation, but she had cut up her dead husband to feed her children; she herself could not eat him. Peter Freuchens, in his *Book of the Eskimos,* tells incredible but true stories of Eskimo women's hardihood, endurance and survival against overwhelming odds. Leo Le Bon, explorer, businessman, and director of Mountain Travel, says that what he has learned from tests conducted by the University of California Physiology Department over twenty-five years, comparing the male and female under stress at high altitude on top of White Mountain in Sierra Nevada, indicates that females function better under stress than males.

Women are physically not so large and strong as men. But with modern lightweight gear and proper training, I think the size difference can be discounted if they prepare themselves for climbing. This book is designed to help the would-be woman climber evaluate her own body, nervous system, and mental capacity for intense activity; to explore the effects of temperature change and altitude on menstruation, and the solutions; to convey basic weather and navigation knowledge, and shortcuts to acquiring mechanical abilities that few women develop in childhood;

to suggest steps and activities that can develop leadership capacity, overcome the natural fear of a new environment, increase confidence, and emphasize the need for constantly improving those traits and the skills of climbing, along with the safety philosophy that is essential for any "life at the top."

2 | THE DECISION

There is liberation for women of fitness, just in the exercise and independence of an expedition, up the side, by hand and foot, of a godward, majestic, phallic beauty. By "her" presence, she feminizes a masculine terrain that is really Mother's Earth.

—C.S. II

There is a group of Polish women climbers who are well known in the elite fraternities and sororities of international climbers—myth-provoking, legendary. I find their will, devotion, *esprit de corps* to be fanatical. From February 21, 1978, for eighteen days, out of Zermatt, these four fought to conquer Mont Cervin's north face (the Matterhorn). Finally, against sixty-mile-per-hour winds and subfreezing temperatures, over rock and ice, Krystyna Palmoroska, thirty years old, an engineer in Poland, reached the summit. It was her second time—she and Anna Czerioinska, a twenty-nine-year-old pharmacist, had climbed the Matterhorn in the summer of 1977. Irene Kessa, a student of twenty-four who was one of their winter climbing comrades, was taken off the mountain by helicopter suffering from serious frostbite. Wanda Rutkiewicz, thirty-five, their leader, plans to join a French and German women's climb in the Himalayas.

To me, they and other dedicated women climbers symbolize the spirit of the women's liberation movement of the 1970s. For these women to succeed at the number-one macho sports activity is the most forceful statement of equality that can be made. Many young women climbers have felt that message. They strive to find other women with whom they can climb. They have had to learn from men on most of these climbs; have been "pulled up" difficult faces; have had to submit to a secondary position; to accept male leadership so often, they are as eager as a corporal hoping a drill sergeant will lose his voice.

Since Billie Jean King humbled Bobby Riggs, women no longer attempt to hide their competitive drive; and mountain climbing, for those with the energy and spirit, has become the perfect bench mark of their determination, fitness and ability. Killing a bull in some *plaza de toros* or outshooting 007 could not be ever so satisfying.

Monica Jackson, married and the mother of two, has climbed extensively in the Alps, the Himalayas, the Atlas Mountains, Great Britain, and Turkish Kurdistan, where she took part in the first *cordée feminine* ascent of Rezko Tepe. She says, " 'Rock ceiling' for women is still being pushed up. . . . There is potentially as much scope for the woman climber of the future as for her male counterpart, and this, if it were not for the arbitrary frontiers imposed by the cruel and absurd exigencies of politics, would still be vast. And, in a sense, the women are better off, because so much is virgin ground for a feminine team. An all-woman ascent of the west face of the Petit Dru or of Everest* would be of great interest both

*An all-woman team climbed Mount Everest in 1975.

scientifically—because of its contribution to our knowledge of physiology—and socially—because of the psychological barrier to be broken down. It is really a question of getting used to the idea. Nobody is surprised when men and women meet on equal terms in horsemanship events, because that has been the historic means of transportation; and riding, therefore, is accepted as a basic human skill."

Then there are those who just want the beauty, the escape, the revitalization, away from the drone of city domestic life. Competition is not in their psyche, even with themselves.

A positive decision is not a commitment carved in stone for a lifetime. Just take a moment's introspection to examine your true interest, to define or create goals and maybe form a purpose, leaving your mind free of doubt to enjoy the action.

If you've bought this book, there is little doubt about your desire. Physical skills may be improved by hard work, but there may be no way of generating desire. You may be motivated by intellectual curiosity, the need to learn. That's enough if you're willing to sweat. As Michael Novak says, "Nothing is more universal than the drive to understand. That drive is endless and is satisfied by nothing on earth. It is the clearest sign in our nature that our home is not here; that we are out of place; and that to be restless and seeking is to be what we most are."

The learning we all strive for in climbing is only partly of nature, rock, snow and ice. It is the hardest of all truths that we really want—the "bottom line" on our own potential, body, wit, heart, emotions. To know "you," you have to learn to push yourself and pace yourself; to learn when to keep loose and easy, when to make demands.

A great mountain is a great gift. How can one extend oneself into fresh heights if there is no peak to lure one higher? When I have tried again and again and still cannot gain the next hold, I feel frustration, fear, even grief, but finally reconciliation. My limits have been extended even when I have retreated.

The recognition of limits is also a form of maturation. With it comes a sense of one's own body and attitudes—a sense, as it were, from the inside out—subtle, luminous and peaceful vibrations from the caverns within that slowly reach the consciousness—a sense of inner unity. Learning how to listen for the core self, the united self is as important for the housewife, the child, or the climber as for the writer.

It was Pythagoras who taught that "we must know the world from the inside, that we can come to know the deeper structure of the universe only through our own body and senses and experiences."

To struggle on the side of a hill with the forces of nature that we understand only incompletely; and with ourselves, whom we know the least, in the beginning, to reach a pointed and pointless objective from which we have to return almost at once may seem to the uninitiated the grandest folly. But how can they know? "Gradient is the elixir of youth," as Jerome Wyckoff so aptly put it.

When I think about the history of mankind's greatness—conspicuous in war, where he has been tested and extended—it is easy to make a case for the equivalency of climbing—not, as some writers do with team sports such as football, as an outlet for aggression and violence, but as a revelation of the best that is in us—courage, endurance, purpose, energies we never knew before, our love of companions; a means of experiencing, if only for a moment, woman as she was meant to be.

As a woman, you may feel guilty about your right to be there. It really is your mountain, too. The only reason you stayed behind "the hunt," nursing baby Homer Erectus and Cro-Magnon, was that your womb was producing the future. Well, the future is now, and it's your earth, too. The ecstasy from gradient and elevated views can be yours!

While on a Himalayan trek in Tibet, upon seeing Annapurna for the first time, sixty-three-year-old Beata Sauerlander said, "Tears came into my eyes, and I put on sunglasses. I am quite unable to talk, and just sit and look. Slowly the clouds move in. I am happier than I can ever remember. The reality of these mountains, their grandeur, the vastness of space surpasses my dreams."

Or, take it from Julian Huxley about his impressions while climbing: "There will come flashes of beauty and of grandeur, light in dark places, sudden glimpses of the age, the glory, and the greatness of the earth."

At altitude, with good cause (and the application of deductive logic), ministers of the 1800s, even in full spirit and robust good health, felt closer to the pearly gates; and later, philosopher Isaac Rosenfeld had his own original explanation of "Why Men Climb": "It has a plain and simple, literal meaning: the impulse, informing all our culture, which has driven the Western world toward the limits of human experience. To stand at the highest point is to occupy such a limit. Here ends the human world—farther one cannot go.

At the limit of our experience are encounters that other worlds of which one can only say the word, that bare being, mere structure, the 'that' of the universe and of God, mountain climbing is the literal metaphor of this encounter."

The godward search for the roofs of our world in outer space must be the single most powerful manifestation of a mystical sign in contemporary life. Climbing drives one upward in some dark and mystical sense, too; it is the manifestation of concern, of will and intellect and passion. Faithful to that concern, the climber will risk great bodily harm, even death—the symbolic death of retreat, only to be born again on the next attempt.

A lifetime on one's derrière, thrilling secondhand to TV or movie excitement, isn't a life at all if the "shoot 'em up" flesh and blood is someone else's. To view someone else's peril, whether we buy or borrow, is an adventure that must fail because it isn't ours. I believe we seek the "exhilaration of fear" because it brings on biochemical changes in us; we become aware of who we are. If "the unexamined life isn't worth living," can the unexperienced life be worth much more?

In another age, the Chinese created an ideograph to represent what we call in English "crisis" by combining two existing characters, the symbol for danger and the symbol for opportunity. Their creation *wei-ji* is the eternal statement that, since opportunity and danger are inseparable, it is impossible to make a significant forward move without a vision of danger; and if danger is sighted, we can sense opportunity and know therefore that we are on the right trail.

Michael Novak states, "The free spirit is not pure

spirit, pure will, pure intellect, pure desire; it is incarnate in hands, and legs and lungs, sinews; in nature at a time, in a season, with others or another like oneself. To choose to move in this direction is to choose against going in *that*. To step forward is to place one foot on a limited bit of [rock]. Without limits, no act, no freedom. Freedom is the art of limits." Climbing is the exercise of freedom.

Feel free to base your decision on practical limits of money and time, but not on trivialities. When you consider that you will be spending your vacation time living out of a backpack; that most of your equipment will last a lifetime; that once you own your own equipment, expense is only food and/or public transportation, you need be only slightly above the national poverty level to afford hiking and climbing. In the beginning, you can borrow or rent much of what you need.

Examine your motives for taking up hiking and climbing. Are you seeking any of the following?

Maturity	New experiences
Learning	Personal discovery
Independence	Health
Self-knowledge	Nature beauty
Social interaction	Group awareness

If the answer is yes to one or all, you're on the way.

Are you hyperactive, nervous?
Are you given to boredom?
Do you fear heights?
Do you fear the dark?
Do you fear snakes?
Do you suffer from claustrophobia?

If your answer is yes to one or all, you have good reason to confront yourself in the most natural way. We could all answer yes at some stage in our lives. With maturity, we find that the difficulties we fear are often much greater than those we actually encounter.

Trivial concerns need to be seriously questioned:

Allergies may affect you only in certain seasons.

Wasp stings may be dangerous to you only in early fall.

Poison ivy is easy to recognize and avoid.

Lower backaches may stem from tension or monthly period and are not necessarily a sign of muscle weakness.

Glasses or contact lenses are no handicap except possibly on record-seeking expeditions.

We all know generally that the best runners have long legs; the best swimmers have broad shoulders; the best basketball players are tall; jockeys are small. We know many exceptions too, so don't eliminate yourself because of physical structure or short-comings. In hiking and climbing there is no best—just those who do and those who stay at home.

Climbing is easier to learn than swimming or horseback riding or tennis. It is basic to our infancy and youth to surmount obstacles in the backyard or park. Who has never climbed a tree or played King of the Hill? It is only the tools and tricks to safely tackle the most difficult challenges that one needs to learn and practice, for otherwise it is child's play.

Women with very large breasts do have special problems with most athletic activities. Fortunately, hiking and climbing are not competitive in the same sense as other sports. Times and scores are not kept. Very large breasts might be a handicap just because they'd be in the way if one's goal is to do serious rock climbing on near-vertical faces. However, a woman's breasts are not easily damaged. Dr. John Marshall, Director of Sports Medicine at Manhattan's Hospital for Special Surgery and the trainer for Billie Jean King, says, "There is no evidence that trauma to the breasts is a precursor of cancer."

There is no reason to fear loss of peak performance because of the menstrual cycle, either. *Time* magazine reports that world and Olympic records have been set by women who were having their periods. Exertion doesn't disrupt the cycle for most women athletes. Very hard training sometimes brings on a cessation of the cycle for a period of months—a condition called amenorrhea. Experts claim that it is due to loss of body fat. This happens to about 45 percent of women who run sixty-five miles a week, and to dancers and gymnasts. A cutback in training and a gain in weight usually restore the normal cycle.

A basic consideration: is your health sufficiently good to allow you to participate in a strenuous sport that requires considerable endurance, often for long periods at higher altitudes than you are accustomed to?

Since one will not start out on Everest, the question that should be put to one's personal physician is, "Do I have your OK to take up hiking and climbing as an activity and to train for it if I start out modestly? That is, gradually?" If the answer is "Yes," begin without future worry. Later, if any problem develops, or if you want to advance to rock climbing or longer expeditions at high altitudes, you can consult your doctor again.

Beware of the male or female doctor whose professional attitude is to play cautious . . . negative in all opinions, especially on subjects about which he or she has little knowledge. I'm not suggesting that if you have some special problem such as diabetes, ulcers, fallen arches, etc., you should ignore the doctor's advice. But there are people, male and female, doctors included, who cannot help reacting with personal bias.

A friend had a chance to ride as an apprentice female jockey for a prominent stable. Her doctor OK'd her general health, but said he thought she was too light boned and would suffer breaks if she fell. My friend was a very experienced horsewoman; that was the reason for the offer. So she knew better than the doctor the dangers involved. Light weight is what makes women ideal jockey material. This doctor had a hard time accepting an attractive "ladylike woman" in a man's work, so he editorialized. A light-boned person is always more susceptible to a break. If everyone's bones were of the same quality (which they are not), a light-boned person would be in more danger of break at any activity—skiing, baseball, etc. One doesn't give up driving an auto because in the event of an accident her light bones are more vulnerable to a break! Some doctors and most men tend to be "crêpe-hangers" anyway; they like to verbalize the grim. Just smile, offer a curt nod, and change the subject.

As you hike and climb, your peak physical condition will increase. You'll learn how to measure your heartbeat and will grow accustomed during training and on the trail to monitoring your exertion. The numbers for your pulse rate can be discussed with your doctor on the phone if you have any concern.

You will become your own doctor, coach, trainer and teacher, but—only in the constructive sense—your own opponent.

In the psychological department, the differences between female and male are many, some obvious; but for expedition mountain climbing, the female seems to be favored. In writing about the medical hazards of the mountain environment, Michael Ward says, "The mental attitude, too, of the female is more directed toward survival than that of the male; though, paradoxically, it is the male who is more likely to get into a survival situation."

Your body was designed as a baby receptacle, with more subcutaneous—under-the-skin—fat for fetus needs, food, heat. Women's estrogens and progesterones are naturally fat producing and fat hoarding hormones. The male needs twice the calories a woman does to sustain his larger muscles. Men burn calories twice as fast for the same exertion. Men use five more calories per pound to maintain themselves than do women. It's like the difference between the gas mileage of a Mack truck and that of a European compact. The female body vehicle burns fuel (fat) more economically than the male body does. You get better mileage. This is a big advantage for any activity that requires endurance, covering ground while carrying weight, often at high altitudes. (This is also why it's harder for women to lose weight.) And that's why you need much more exercise than you ever imagined.

The "Catch 22" is that you have to learn how to use your advantage. Your body may or may not have the horsepower needed to handle a strenuous workload, but that's not a design fault. If you have not been an active athlete up to now, you can still build and improve your motor—your cardiovascular system—with training. Age is absolutely no barrier to increasing the capacity of your heart—your motor. Any exercise good for the heart will also improve lung capacity. The body runs on fat calories and oxygen, and one needs the complete system to get the most mileage.

Mountain climbing as a hobby is not just a weekend or vacation activity. To be enjoyed to the fullest, it's a full-time preoccupation. Your physical training, diet and life-style between "mountain times" are vital to the success you will experience on expeditions. Try not to look on training as a price you must pay for the fun of being in the mountains once in a while. Rather, make it your goal to gain the greatest development possible with the raw material nature has given you. There is no guarantee of "ninety days and parts" or a trade-in allowance on your body if you think you've got a lemon. It's the only one you'll ever get, so you'd better make the most of it. Of course the same is true of your mind. Climbing is the one single sport I know of that can help you reach your full potential in both body and mind.

The upper-body strength of a man is generally greater for the same body weight than for a woman. If a man and a woman of the same weight compare arm strength, the man will usually be stronger. Don't let that negative cause you concern. It is not upper-body strength that makes climbers! The big muscles of the legs get the most use. Even on rock climbing, pulling yourself up with the arms is a bad technique and is to be avoided. It uses too much energy and causes early fatigue. It's the big muscles of the thighs that take you up. Backpack weight rests on the hips, not the back; the shoulder straps are mainly for balance. Women, because of their more pronounced hip slope, have an advantage that men lack. The backpack belt causes less friction and need not be so tight to hold, allowing free blood circulation and greater comfort. It helps to have strong hands and arms, but it's a simple matter of exercise. If you'll tune in to ABC on any Saturday afternoon, you may see some women's gymnastic competition. These contests display the superlative strength and balance of the young women athletes. They certainly have superior arm and body strength for handstands and tumbling.

Put to rest that ancient misconception of our mothers. Women who exercise do not develop muscles like Mr. America's. You can increase your strength without acquiring a muscular look. "The female body composition is only 23 percent muscle, in contrast to 40 percent for the male," Dr. Jack Wilmore, president of the American College of Sport Medicine, says. "Women, because they have low levels of androgenic hormones that enlarge muscles, can increase their strength 50 percent to 75 percent with no increase in muscle bulk."

I believe that women in general have a better sense of balance than men. The gadget in our inner ears that makes riding a surfboard possible may be more finely tuned in women than in men. I say this only from my own observation of dancers and gymnasts.

The greatest handicap a woman has in any form of athletics is visualizing herself in that role. This is especially true of mountain climbing, given the weight of precedent that, traditionally, hiking, climbing and other activities of the great outdoors are the

province of the sacred macho world. But human beings are very adaptable. Once we see examples, we
follow. After the TV appearance of Olga Korbut in
the Olympics, girls took to gymnastics as easily as to
the hula hoop. Young female America had their role
model.

On the other hand, there doesn't exist a female
climbing super-hero, because it's sort of an anti-hero
sport. Climbers don't consider it a sport anyway, but
rather an art, like sculpturing or leatherwork, in the
sense that a person works a route in her own individual style—more like cooking or a craft than vol-
leyball. It is not competitive—you are your only
competitor—and it is not covered in the sports pages.
All of which may be a blessing, because there is no one
super she-jock to give beginners any feeling of
inferiority.

A woman can be strong without being muscular;
knowledgeable about weather, terrain and ropes
without being a cowgirl. Femininity will still be on
your dressing table when you return indoors. The
soft, feminine side of your nature, combined with the
inner strength of confidence that comes from realistic
self-knowledge, can make mature happiness a vital
part of a secure woman's personality. "Exercise puts
sparkle in a woman's eyes and pink in her cheeks, and
creates a physical vitality that almost bursts out," says
Dr. Joan Ullyot. "She becomes body-centered and
very sensual."

Woman's greatest physical weakness with respect to
any form of athletics is her feet. Training cannot
begin until you have bought your boots, so begin by
reading the chapter on Outfitting, make boots your
first purchase, and wear them throughout the training

period. Stiff "high tops" are necessary to support the feet and ankles while carrying the added weight for expedition hikes or climbing. Your feet are not used to the confinement and the rigidity necessary for safety. But you'll be able to condition them by wearing the boots every day, as well as to break in the boots as recommended on page 81.

Running, too, will be an important part of your training. A lot of women I know dislike running intensely. If they were heavy breasted, that would seem to be a good reason. It wouldn't be fun carrying that extra weight around. But slim girls sometimes have an aversion to running, too. My belief is that they expected too much in the beginning, then became discouraged because they couldn't go very far and developed aches and pains right away. If you have not been active competitively in some form of athletics on a regular basis for a year or more, you must take the time to build up endurance gradually. If you do this, there will be no pain; only satisfaction.

I know some of you will say, "Not for me. I don't want to be out there with all those show-off female jocks in the park. I just wanted to find a sport to get away from the crowd. If I've got to do a lot of running, it's not for me." If, after reading this book, hiking and climbing intrigue you as much as when you bought it, take my word that all those hesitations about running can be solved; most important of all, your first hiking trip or expedition will be a guaranteed success because you've taken the precaution of conditioning and thus have eliminated the chance of a strain or pain that would surely spoil your maiden outing and might possibly discourage future attempts. Jogging and running are the basics of all conditioning for endurance. Nearly all competitive athletes run to build up endurance and wind. Boxers do ten to twelve miles of roadwork a day to be able to go fifteen rounds in a fight. Even the European Ping-Pong champion runs three miles a day.

On November 14, 1977, *Newsweek* reported that 500,000 women now run or jog regularly! *Sports Illustrated* reported that 619 females ran in the 1977 Honolulu Marathon, the greatest number to ever run a marathon of twenty-seven miles. Ninety-five percent finished!

Dr. Marshall claims that the biggest problem women have is lack of adequate training. He also says, "A woman in good shape, however, will outdistance male competitors in those rare races of fifty miles or more because they burn fuel more efficiently." Dr. Ullyot comments on women running: "If a woman and a man are running at their own pace, a woman can generally go farther than the man with the same amount of training."

Running is the quickest, most economical means of building up wind and heart and, for women particularly, strengthening and toughening the feet. But it is not the test of your future abilities as a climber. There are some expert climbers who are very poor runners. You don't have to become a fleet-footed marathoner to get the conditioning benefits—a pony gets just as much exercise by running as a racehorse does. In combination with other activities in a consistent routine, daily running for fourteen days will prepare you for the first expedition. If one is older or overweight, training may take from thirty to sixty days; but there's no shame in that. You've just had to come from farther back. Your pride and satisfaction will be even greater once you reach that first summit. Do the training by yourself, and no one will know how bad you were in the beginning. You'll then be able to hold your own with any group on the trail. As Beverly Johnson, after her solo climb of El Capitan, said to her interviewers in answer to the question, "What did you think about for nine days?": "I thought about the question, 'How do you eat an elephant?' The answer is, 'You eat it one bite at a time.'"

3 | PLACES TO GO

A woman's place is on top.
> —Motto of the American Women's
> Annapurna Expedition, 1979

What every woman needs first is a mountain—one of
her own—to "fix on," plan for, fantasize about.*
Yours can be real, out of the pages of books, glimpsed
from an airplane, or imagined—just so you have a
mental picture of the object of your affection. It's not
the mountain you train on. It's usually not near your
home. My first mountain was the Matterhorn. That
was the one I climbed in 1948. Later, it became the
Grand Teton in Wyoming. Now the one I think about,
read about, talk about, and one day will climb is Cerro
Torre in Patagonia. Your own boots and your own
mountain: those are the first things; all the rest follows.

There are many more mountains than boots to
choose from, and in reality lots of time to decide. But
to consider the inventory, take a look at the world

---

*Women—especially the artistic, it seems—are naturally
prone to choose their own mountains even if not to climb. A
Massachusetts group of women poets chose the Tibetan name
for Mount Everest, Chomo Uri, which means "Mother of the
Turquoise Peak," for the name of their periodical.

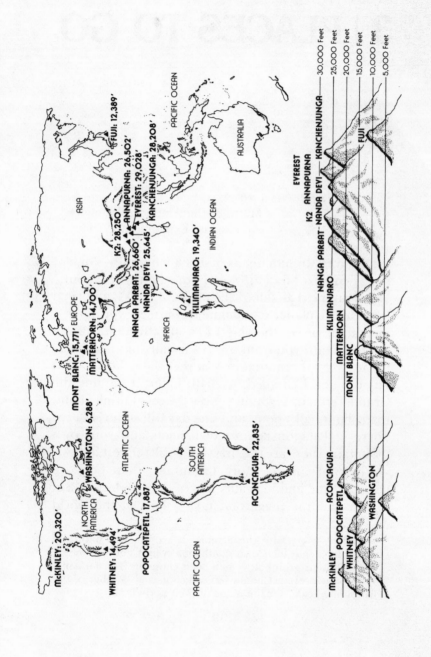

Above: Huayna Potosi in Bolivia.

Below: Ganesh Himalaya.

map. Anthony Huxley, who edited the *Standard Ency-clopedia of the World's Mountains*, listed 2,378 major peaks, passes and ranges, with contrasting names like Tobacco Root Mountain, Montana; Rabbit Ears, Har-vard, and Troublesome mountains in Colorado; or Iconoclast and Jumbo mountains in British Columbia. But nothing beats the brevity and rhythm of Api, Bun La, Bam La, or Ha La—unless it's Buz Dag or Bab Dog—all in Nepal, India, Tibet, Bhutan, Turkey, or Azerbaijan SSR. Many mountains have been given feminine names, such as Gylamo Chen, which means Great Queen.

It is a fact that one-fourth of the earth's land area is considered mountainous—that is, over 3,000 feet above sea level—and covering 14 million square miles are mountains that are high and cold enough to be above the permanent snowline. In the eastern United States we have the Green Mountains, the White Mountains, the Adirondacks, the Catskills, the Berk-shires, the Poconos, the Alleghenies, the Blue Ridge Mountains, and the Great Smokies—each a major mountain group, each a segment of the Appala-chians. In the Rockies there are over a hundred large mountain ranges, each with its own name.

The Appalachian chain reaches from Alabama into the hills of Newfoundland, with Mount Mitchell in the Blue Ridge of the Great Smokies in North Carolina being the highest peak east of the Mississippi—6,684 feet. Forty-three peaks in the Smokies reach to 6,000 feet. Harney Peak, 7,242 feet, in the Black Hills of South Dakota is the highest point east of the Rockies. As we work our way west, the granddaddies of the United States are Pikes Peak, 14,110 feet, and Mount Elbert, 14,431 feet, in Colorado; but Mount Whitney in California goes 64 feet taller—14,495 feet—the highest in the United States. Now imagine another Mount Whitney stacked on top of the existing one, and you approach the height of Mount Everest. Himalayan peaks begin where American peaks leave off: fourteen peaks of 26,250 feet or more. Tibet has an average height of over 16,000 feet, including a plateau 1,000 miles wide that is higher than any U.S. peak. Altitude is relative except with respect to breathing. Even Kansas, the flattest of the states, has its own Mount Sunflower, a mighty 4,039 feet above sea level. It must seem to tower over the surrounding plains at 3,500 feet. The awe of altitude depends on the elevation where the viewer is standing, whether he's looking up or down, and whether he is contemplating the trip or has already arrived.

Anyway, it isn't altitude above sea level you need for the climbing experience; it is good rock and gradient. As you read about climbers, you'll notice that most began at home. Perish any misconceptions that one must live in Switzerland, Nepal, or Colorado to get into mountain climbing. Whymper, who first climbed the Matterhorn in 1865, began in the Lake district of his native England. Hilary, first on Mount Everest in 1953, accompanied by Tenzing Norgay, a Sherpa, began mountain climbing in his native New Zealand. The Japanese, who have achieved many record climbs outside their own country, practice on tall buildings and seaside cliffs.

Eastern United States

WHITE MOUNTAINS. There are three White Mountain ranges in the U.S. The White Mountains in New Hampshire are the most extensive and best known:

1,000 square miles in area, all part of the great Appalachian system—a profusion of peaks, notches and ravines in the 4,000-foot class, the highest being Mount Washington, 6,288 feet. Lots of good granite rock climbing, easily accessible from the Boston area.

THE ALLEGHENIES go from north-central Pennsylvania into southwestern Virginia and southern West Virginia. They are rugged near-wilderness, with great gorges cut through mountains by the Potomac and New rivers near Spruce Knob in West Virginia (4,860 feet). Good for short hiking excursions, weekend outings.

THE ADIRONDACKS are in northeastern New York State. They include the Algonquin, 5,112 feet, and the second largest forest preserve in the U.S., centered in a mountain area. There is year-round hiking and rock climbing. To learn about rock climbing, read the Adirondack Mountain Club's *A Climber's Guide to the Adirondacks* by Trudy Healy, published in 1971. It costs $3.00 and can be purchased by writing to the club at R.D. 1, Ridge Road, Glen Falls, New York 12801. This area and this guidebook make an excellent combination for trying a first guideless or solo or all-woman beginner party. Maps and highway markers show how to find a particular spot. Grade information, degree of difficulty, and technical instructions are complete and include photos and diagrams of routes. The club holds annual beginner sessions at Heart Lake and welcomes rank beginners. The rock is not so good as that in the Shawangunks, which is the best in the east, but the climbing area is spread wide. The first recorded climb was on Mount Colden via the trap dike route in July 1850. Interestingly, John C. Case, a former president of the American

Alpine Club, and Betty Woolsey, who was later captain of the first Olympic ski team, made the first ascent of Mount Wallface in August 1933.

SHAWANGUNKS. Here is the best rock climbing in New York, near New Paltz and the famous Mohonk Hotel (over one hundred years old) and two hours from New York City. On summer weekends, trucks sell hot dogs, lobsters and clams. A small cataract of gray cliffs, 350 feet at most, 393 routes, some "white knucklers." The climbing area is extensive, over 2½ miles long, with climbs ranging from grades 5.0 to 5.13. The most enjoyable climbs are rated at 5.3–5.6, and there are many in this category. The hard rock is quartz conglomerate, steep with overhangs. One needs permission from a ranger. A daily permit costs about $1.50; annual permit, $18.00; this includes climbing, hiking, biking, camping. Copies of an old and out of print but very good guidebook are available through instructor John Ross (914–658–9811). A new guidebook, released in the spring of 1979, is available at the local climbing headquarters: Rock & Snow, 44 Main Street, New Paltz, New York 12561. Manager Harvey Arnold and Dick Williams serve free advice generously, as well as directions and expensive climbing accessories.

BLUE RIDGE MOUNTAINS. Located in southern Pennsylvania and into Georgia, the highest being Grandfather Mountain, which is 5,964 feet. The famous Appalachian Trail follows much of the range on top of the ridge. Good for lengthy expedition hiking in the spring and fall.

CATSKILL MOUNTAINS. In Greene, Ulster and Delaware counties in New York State, these reach a peak of 4,204 feet on Slide Mountain. This is Rip Van

Winkle country with some good year-round trails for beginners.

THE GREEN MOUNTAINS stretch from Massachusetts to Quebec, right through the center of Vermont, and extend the length of the state. Mount Mansfield, 4,393 feet, is the highest. The Long Trail, 260 miles, is marked and maintained and has sleeping shelters and fireplaces for great hiking summer and fall; there is some rock climbing. Easy access from roads makes short or long trips possible. *Guide Book of Long Trail*, published by the Green Mountain Club, P.O. Box 94, Rutland, Vermont 05701, was only $3.00 in 1971 when I hiked in the Mount Mansfield and Stowe areas. This is the finest guidebook I've ever seen; it makes trips for beginners a secure pleasure. Long Trail is ideal for first-experience hiking without a local guide; no need for tents or stoves. One must travel in large groups of four or five to have comfortable security when meeting others on the trail.

Midwestern United States

OZARK MOUNTAINS. Located in Missouri, Arkansas and Oklahoma, these go up to 2,500 feet and cover over 50,000 square miles; good woods hiking, rocky cliffs in places for rock climbing, and plenty of minerals, furry animals, and freshwater fish.

OUACHITA MOUNTAINS. A series of east-west ridges up to 2,900 feet high in eastern Oklahoma and western Arkansas, explored by Hernando de Soto about 1541. The Rich Mountains in Oklahoma begin at Little Rock, Arkansas, and extend 220 miles west to Atoka, Oklahoma—rugged, rocky pine and oak covered. Home of famous Hot Springs, which, together with North, West and Sugar Loaf mountains, lies within the National Park of 1,019 acres. Hiking, camping, some rock climbing.

Western United States

WHITE MOUNTAINS. Those of eastern Arizona lie in the Fort Apache Indian Reservation and boast Green Peak, 10,115 feet, and Baldy Peak, 11,590. This third range of White Mountains is shared by California and Nevada. The highest peak in California rises to 14,242 feet; Boundary Peak, the highest point in Nevada, rises to 13,145 feet.

THE ROCKY MOUNTAINS run from central New Mexico through Colorado, Utah, Idaho and Montana to the Canadian border, with peaks as high as 14,000 feet; referred to as the Continental Divide. Sixty-five peaks exceed 10,000 feet, helping to make Colorado the mountain-climbing capital of the United States. The University of Colorado at Boulder has more climbing enthusiasts than McDonald has hamburgers. This is the only place I have overheard luncheonette conversation about a "Boxx Belay," "Chimney Stuck," "Up a crevasse without crampons." And they talk of climbing the way old jocks talk of football in the bar-room. Every student wears a carabiner on his belt buckle to hold pitons as well as keys. In classrooms you see summit packs used to carry books and tennis rackets. "Peak baggers" abound; one carries his own journal and is trying for thirty-five climbs of over 10,000 feet before graduation. The university is also the center for women climbers. Boulder, Colorado, and Berkeley in California have the highest concentration of women climbers.

Another great center for climbing in the Rockies is Jackson Hole, Wyoming. There, 13,000-foot Grand Teton is America's answer to the postcard-perfect Swiss Matterhorn, an unsurpassed vertical cone across "buffalo flats" to the east. Climbing combines expedition conditions in winter and challenging walls for rock climbing. Guides and training classes are available.

Not far to the southeast is Gannett Peak, 13,785 feet, the highest in the state. It is located at the northern end of the Wind River range, with its glaciers, alpine meadows and snow-capped peaks. At the southern end, the town of Lander, Wyoming, is headquarters for the National Outdoor Leadership School founded by the legendary American climber Paul Petzoldt. NOLS and Colorado Outward Bound in Denver have baptized nearly half of the women hikers and climbers in the United States today. The Tetons and the Wind Rivers get a four-star rating for climbing and hiking if you have a minimum of ten days.

In northern Wyoming and southern Montana, the Big Horn Mountains, with 13,165-foot Cloud Peak, are still part of the Rockies. Rugged erosion exposes granite and small glaciers; the upper reaches are forested, and lakes and wildlife resemble a western movie setting. This is a good summer spot for hiking and climbing.

In Wyoming's northeast corner, the famous Devils Tower, used as the visual symbol and landmark for UFOs in the movie *Close Encounters of the Third Kind*, stands only 865 feet from its base; but for generations of hikers and climbers it has been one of this country's most intriguing challenges. In spite of its seeming impregnability and near-vertical sides, it has been climbed often on every face, with the use of pitons. Eighty-one ascents were made during a "Mountaineer's Week" in 1956. Today no one can keep count. Devils Tower would be an interesting place to try a novice all-woman rock climb.

Pacific Western United States

CASCADE MOUNTAINS. In the Pacific West we have the Cascade range, which extends from British Columbia to Oregon, Washington and California, reaching up to 14,408 feet at Mount Rainier, 700 miles long, north from Lassen Peak in California.

Mount Rainier is a dormant volcano with the largest single-peak glacier system in the United States. It is part of the national park of the same name and has twenty-six great glaciers, five of which originate on the summit of Mount Rainier. Other giant glaciers, born of snow in rock pockets or cirques, are: Carbon, Cowlitz, Fryinjsan, Puyallup and Russell. Myriad streams from melting glaciers feed belts of wildflowers. At 5,400 feet, a 50-mile belt of flowers encircles the mountain. There are 75 miles of road and 276 miles of trail. Climbing on ridges of crumbling lava and pumice and along inclined and crevassed ice fields can be difficult and unpleasant. The ascent is usually made from Paradise Valley or White River, and climbers must register with the park ranger, who will question and examine hikers and climbers to determine "satisfactory evidence of their physical abilities, knowledge and experience in hazardous climbing and possession of proper equipment."

Mount Shasta, 14,162 feet, is in northern California.

The Shasta Indians believed that their mountain stood at the dawn of creation, the sole point of land sticking up out of the primordial ocean. Since the Eocene epoch, occurring about 58 million years ago on the geological time scale and characterized by the rise of the mammals, periodic upsurges of viscous lava have pushed through the cone, which is almost perfectly symmetrical in form, and flowed over the surrounding country, sometimes hardening in crusts over the still-molten lava below. The mountain built up slowly until it towered 10,000 feet above the countryside, a giant cone 80 cubic miles in volume, coated by the last eruption a few centuries ago, with a surface of pumice and ash three to four inches deep. This, plus porus lava below, absorbs the snow and glacier-melt waters of today. These waters issue from the mountain base as gigantic springs, each pouring forth hundreds of cubic feet of water per second, mostly into Pit River, the largest tributary of the Sacramento. There are many stories and Indian legends about light phenomena, ghosts, and wizards who caused avalanches and hurled boulders down the slope. Mount Shasta is an easy mountain to climb, with a glorious view in every direction from the ultimate 400-foot pinnacle revealing a striking panorama across a snow plateau, from the crumbling crater wall to the subsidiary 12,433-foot cone of the Shastines and the acid lava plain below. Very interesting expedition outing—mostly hiking and backpacking.

THE OLYMPIC GROUP, on the Olympic Peninsula in northwestern Washington, includes 1,313.8 square miles of national park 50 miles west of Seattle. It has seven large glaciers. It is the recipient of abundant rainfall; it abounds in great trees 200 to 300 feet high—Alaska cedar, juniper and Douglas fir—and gigantic Roosevelt elk. Summer and winter hiking expeditions can be very adventurous. Mount Olympus, 7,954 feet, is its main mountain.

SIERRA NEVADA, a range dividing the central valley from the Great Basin, is located in eastern California. It includes Mount Whitney, 14,495 feet, the highest mountain in the United States; reaches more than 400 miles southeast from the Cascade range to Tehachapi Pass southeast of Bakersfield; encompasses three great national parks: Yosemite, Kings Canyon, and Sequoia, with their striking gorges of the Kern, Kings, Merced and Tuolumne rivers, the spectacular Yosemite Falls, and others; granite monoliths like Half Dome; and many glacial lakes and meadows of striking beauty. Forming the highest portion are the High Sierras, located south of Lake Tahoe and partly in Nevada, between the main chain and the Carson range. Mount Williamson, 14,384 feet; Mount Langley, 14,042 feet; Mount Tyndall, 14,025 feet; Mount Muir, 14,025 feet; and Mount Barnard, 14,003 feet, give the Bay Area climbers every challenge for practicing rock, ice or expedition climbing.

Yosemite National Park in east-central California has peaks rising to 13,090 feet—Mount Lyell—and 13,055 feet—Mount Dana—on the eastern boundary of the park. The most famous climbing mountains at the 6,000- to 10,000-foot level are El Capitan, 7,564 feet; Half Dome, 8,852 feet (an immense split monolith with a vertical face of 2,000 feet); Clouds Rest Peak, 9,930 feet; Cathedral Rocks, 6,531 feet; and, close by, the Cathedral Spires. The Grand Canyon of the Tuolumne River is mile-deep in places and includes Hetch Hetchy valley, with Hetch Hetchy

Dome, 6,200 feet, rising above it. It is the home of a series of beautiful waterfalls during May and June, some of them drying up in the late summer. Upper Yosemite Falls plunges 1,430 feet, and Lower Yosemite Falls 320 feet—"equal to eleven Niagaras." There is Ribbon Falls, 1,612 feet, one of the highest single cataracts in the world, and half a dozen more of spectacular beauty.

In the variety of its beauty, Yosemite surpasses Switzerland. Words cannot convey the true emotional reaction one experiences, or even describe the sights accurately enough. In Anthony Huxley's words, "The falls form a ring descending from the great precipices that encircle the flat lush green meadowlands and woods of the broad valley, from an upland region of vast granite peaks and domes which slopes from the glaciers and snows of the Sierra Nevada. These uplands strike a wonderful contrast to the luxuriance of the level valley floor with its rich clay soil . . . miles of undulating country, of silver gray granite, deep cut here and there by rivers (and by glaciers in the Ice Age), clothed with dense coniferous forests, where the soil is deep and varied by innumerable lakes, tarns and streams. In the high country, there are stretches of sub-alpine meadows, vivid green and dotted with innumerable flowers." Perfect for a group of girls or women to spend a month of camping, hiking and rock climbing, though crowded in summer. Lots of assistance nearby—luxury lodges if one needs or wants them. If you could choose only one place to climb and see in your lifetime, this would have to be it.

4 | TRAINING

> [*There is*] *a new female recognition (something men have always known) that there are important lessons to be learned from sports competition, among them that winning is the result of hard, sustained, serious training, cool clear strategy that includes the use of tricks and bluffs, and a positive mind-set that puts all reflex systems on "go." This knowledge, and the chances to put it into practice, is precisely what women have been conditioned to abjure.*
>
> —Susan Brownmiller
> *Against Our Will*

Training for mountain climbing means stretching, running, and strengthening exercises performed in a disciplined, purposeful routine, simultaneously monitored for your "body talk." Learning to sense warning signals from slight pains, stiffness, or fatigue is a basis for getting to know your physical self; a start on the mental frame of knowledge of your whole person during expeditions, ascents—and a lifetime.

In this chapter, I have outlined a special fourteen-day training program to prepare you both physically and mentally for the twenty-four-hour demands of a first expedition. It is important not to miss a day, whether rain or shine, when doing your fourteen consecutive days of training. Remember, on an expedition there are no breaks.

It's advisable to do the two-week training at least a month ahead of a scheduled trip, because circumstances may cause an interruption of the training period, and you may be forced to start over.

If you do finish with time to spare, and if you feel confident that your endurance and strength are sufficiently good and that your boots and your feet are broken in, continue the training on an alternate-day schedule.

Breaking in Your Boots

At the first opportunity, you will want to put on your hiking boots and go out for a fast-paced walk on good ground—not concrete. When you return, change into tennis sneakers and try walking and jogging equal amounts—100 yards each over the same route you just walked. That one-hour experience will tell you a lot about the condition of your feet and your shoes. The climbing shoes will feel stiff and heavy. You'll find it more tolerable to break in your boots gradually over a period of weeks.

Stretching

The stretch is the key to all extended physical activity and is a great revitalizer, both mentally and physically.

Most women I've observed already have good flexibility—although good natural flexibility does not eliminate the need for stretching as a regular routine if one is to be physically active. The exceptions are those who wear heels continually. This usually shortens the hamstrings, and these women have trouble stretching hands to toes with the knees straight; nor can they hold that position for any length of time.

Not long ago my son and I planned a short weekend hike on the Long Trail. His twenty-eight-year-old girlfriend in New York City wanted to make the trip with us. I agreed, but insisted that she do some jogging in advance. I was thinking as much of him as of her, for I knew that the city had softened his resolve to stay in shape, and I guessed she'd insist that he accompany her in the park. She did!

Our hike was great fun going out. We were on the way back and were about halfway down a steep grade, each carrying a small load, when my son's friend began to camplain of pain in her legs below the knees, on the shins. We'd been going downhill at rather a fast pace, so we broke to rest. On resuming our hike, after the first few yards she complained that her shins hurt even more. Massaging the sore muscles didn't seem to help. In fact, the pressure of our fingers brought tears to her eyes. We were a long way from the car—maybe five miles. Fortunate for us the trail was wide and smooth, even though steep. My son and I, each holding one of her arms for support, walked her backwards all the way to the bottom. Only in this position did she feel no strain or pain on the shin muscles.

During the drive back to the city she told me that because she was so short she had worn high heels since she was thirteen years old—fifteen years of unnatural foot position! My son and she are no longer together but I still hear from her occasionally. She now wears flats at home and in the office but heels on the street. Being a perfectionist, she has also gone to a specialist for therapy to correct the weakness in the shin muscles and does strengthening exercises at home. And she has taken new boy friends on the same trail without any complaint. That is, *she* doesn't complain; some of the men do!

To achieve the great energy that comes from stretching, one must learn to find that midpoint between the easy stretch and the drastic stretch. Only with this awareness can one realize the potential for revitalizing the body. If the stretch is too easy, it becomes boring, and there is no conscious awareness of the feeling of a stretch—no energy gain. If you stretch too far, you will not be able to relax enough during the stretch to feel the body extend; besides, overstretching can cause injury and thus break the routine.

Somewhere between the two extremes is the correct personal stretch for *your* body, muscles and tendons that will allow the development of awareness, energy, strength and enjoyment. Stretching becomes natural and effortless when done regularly and with the correct attitude; there is no need for hard-driving discipline.

A good stretch should start with twenty to thirty seconds of holding the stretch while concentrating on relaxation. Follow with what Bob Anderson calls the "developmental stretch" for more than thirty seconds. Allow the feeling of the stretch to become more intense, without allowing it to reach the point of pain. A drastic stretch is counterproductive.

Remember:

Don't bounce when you stretch.
Don't strain to the point of pain.
Do relax.

Do breathe rhythmically.
Do stretch before and after a workout or running.

BACK STRETCH. Bend over from the waist, keeping your legs straight.

Let your head and arms hang loosely. Relax, letting gravity pull your back and leg tendons. Maintain the position for one minute. Swing briefly from side to side. Repeat three or four times.

CALF STRETCH. Stand three feet from and facing a wall or post. Keeping your feet flat on the floor, lean forward, supporting yourself with your hands. For greater effect, bend one knee and put the other foot farther back, toe pointed toward the wall; lock that knee straight and flatten your heel on the ground, so that you can feel the stretching behind the calf. Alternate legs two or three times, holding for thirty seconds or more.

DANCER'S STRETCH. Using a table, railing or shelf about waist high, put one foot up, keeping your knees straight, and bend your body down over your outstretched leg. Reach toward your toes with your hands. Grip your ankle or foot and stretch until you can feel the pull in the back of your thigh. If possible, "lie down" along the horizontal leg. Hold your farthest position for thirty seconds or more; then repeat with the other leg.

TRUNK STRETCH. Put your hands on your waist and bend forward slightly from the waist. Keeping your back straight, slowly describe a circle with the top part of your body, clockwise. Concentrate on stretching your side, back and stomach muscles. Repeat five to six times, then reverse direction.

Outdoor Stretches

Here are stretches that are good for
doing out of doors. Take the positions
shown in the sketches and hold for as
long as comfortable.

FLOOR KICK. Lie on your back, with legs together on the floor and arms outstretched at the sides. Keeping your upper body flat, roll your hips to the left and slowly kick your right foot up along floor above your outstretched left hand. Return your right foot below your body and repeat in the other direction, kicking your left foot above your outstretched right hand. This exercise helps to loosen the vertebrae of the spine, as well as to stretch the hamstrings.

YOGA ONE LEG. Sit on the floor with your legs stretched out in front. Bend your left knee and bring your left foot up to your crotch. Reach forward with both hands along your straight right leg as far as possible. Grasping your ankle or foot, bend at the waist and attempt to touch your right knee with your face. Hold for thirty seconds, consciously tightening that knee to feel a pull on the back of your leg. Reverse the leg position and repeat for thirty to sixty seconds. Alternate four or five times.

Also study the twelve stretches illustrated on the preceding pages.

Strengthening Exercises

Repetition is the important factor in strengthening any set of muscles. Do the exercises five or six times correctly, then later, do them five or six times more. If you can manage only two or three repeats, try for two or three more within an hour. Just add to the total attempts each day, and your strength will increase as if by magic.

When you've become an experienced hiker and climber and are sufficiently strong, it will be better to do your strengthening exercises every other day, running on the alternate day.

HAND STRENGTHENER. Get a racketball—made of soft and springy rubber—and squeeze with each hand for three to five minutes several times a day.

SHIN STRENGTHENER. Using a chair with a straight back, sit six inches from the back. Extend your legs in front of you. Place the heel of one foot on the toes of the other. Pull the toes back up against the heel, while resisting with the heel. Contract the bottom foot completely back, then relax it flat again. Do this six to twelve times twice a day.

WRIST STRENGTHENER. While seated, rest your forearm on a horizontal surface with your hand extended palm up, knuckles bent, over the edge. Extend the other arm, elbow stiff, and grip the palm and knuckles of the lower hand. Push the lower hand upward in a full arc while resisting with the straight arm; then let it relax and return. Reverse the lower arm so that the knuckles are upward and repeat. Do this six to twelve times twice a day.

PUSHUPS. Hold your body horizontal and rigid above the floor, supported on your toes and palms, with your elbows straight. Lower your body by bending your elbows until your chin touches the floor, then return to your starting position. If you can do this ten to twelve times, you're very strong. If you cannot do more than two or three repetitions, follow them with ten repetitions done with your knees on the floor.

CHIN-UPS. For a chinning bar, look around your neighborhood. There may be a convenient tree limb nearby at the right height—or you can stand on a box platform. Rough bark helps prevent slipping, but it's best not to use branches that are more than three inches in diameter. If the limb bends, move nearer the tree trunk. If you live in the city, you may have to purchase a doorway chinning bar. These are sold at all sporting goods dealers from $10 to $20, but they will last a lifetime and will double as clothes hangers. Check the width of your doorframe before buying. They are not complicated to install. Get your building super or a "heavy" boy friend to test it if you're in doubt about its strength.

The most effective chin-up is done on a bar at a height that allows you to grasp it with your arms fully extended and feet not touching the floor. Your hands should be shoulder width apart on the bar. While bending your elbows, pull your chin up above the bar; then return to a full extension. Do a set with your knuckles facing you and a set with them facing away. Six in a set is ideal; if you can manage that many, you're sufficiently strong for a beginning climber. If you can do no more than two, use a stool or bench to partially support your legs through five or six more repetitions.

FENCER'S SPLIT. Stand with your legs wide apart, your hands on your hips. Turn your left toes so that they point left and rotate your hips in the same direction. Slowly bend your left knee until your buttock touches the heel of your left foot, keeping your right leg straight the whole time. Return to starting position and repeat the exercise with your right leg.

BENT-KNEE SIT-UPS. Lie on the floor, knees bent, with your hands behind your head. Hook your toes under a piece of heavy furniture or have a roommate anchor your feet. Raise your torso slowly from the waist, feeling each vertebra. Touch your knees with your elbows. Roll back smoothly until your hands rest on the floor. Repeat twenty-five to thirty times. Do this exercise two to three times during a workout period.

Running

Your body runs on oxygen, the most important nutritional element for the 60 billion cells in your body. A person will die within a few minutes if the brain is deprived of oxygen.

If you are seated or lying, you use seven to nine quarts of air (containing a total of approximately half a pint of oxygen) per minute. Walking increases the per-minute consumption to a pint and a half of oxygen; but jogging—that is, running at a speed just faster than your fastest walking rate—requires two quarts of oxygen per minute, for a total breathing volume of forty-five quarts of air. This eightfold increase in oxygen consumption, when channeled through the body for one-half to one hour each day, will guarantee a healthy heart, lungs and nervous system, giving you the capacity to hike and climb at high altitudes.

Before running, you should always do warm-up exercises. Find a comfortable floor space in your house, preferably with a carpet or pad to cushion the body. Do a number of stretching exercises to warm up your system and to stretch the tendons and muscles of the legs, as well as those of the back and shoulders.

For running, wear loose-fitting long pants and a large shirt. Unless it is summer, any old cottons will do. In bad weather, add hat, gloves, and waterproof outer garments. There's nothing wrong with running in a raincoat. Don't waste money on fashionable warm-up suits. These are usually no good in foul weather and only attract the attention of pedestrians. Spend the extra money for better boots.

Avoid wearing a bra that is too tight. Rigorous arm motion often causes restricted circulation in the arms, which can result in swelling. The best bra for running is a bikini top that's designed for swimming. It gives support around the neck, and the absence of a tight body strap allows arm action. Running without a bra can be very comfortable, but there is the danger of rough shirt material rubbing your nipples raw from the friction. As a precaution, use Vaseline on both of the nipples and cover with tape.

Your first choice of a running location should be a college or high school track or a grassy infield or park. If you're shy, run after dark; there's less likelihood of being annoyed by loudmouths. Wear white, carry a small flashlight, and put fluorescent tape on your jacket, front and back (buy it at any auto supply store). Run facing traffic if you're in the street, and shine your flashlight at oncoming cars.

Time yourself with a watch that has a second hand; if possible, take a friend along the first few days to help time you. Jog 300 yards in two to two and a half minutes, then walk 100 yards. If breathing is painful or you are too winded, divide that distance and jog 150 yards and walk 50 (a city block is about 100 yards). Repeat four or five times, then add one repetition every second day until you reach eleven or twelve. If no soreness occurs, try to run a mile without stopping; then do the jog-walk. Work up to half an hour or three miles. After you have become an experienced hiker and climber, your goal should be to jog one hour every other day. When you're able to do that without any soreness, try to run more distance in one hour. When you're doing six miles or more in an hour, you're ready to climb above 15,000 feet.

The important thing to know about your heart is that its recovery rate is the significant indicator of a healthy cardiovascular system. If your heart rate returns to below 120 within five minutes after exercising, you are in no danger. To push yourself to greater training once your muscles are conditioned, you need to know your maximum training rate, which you can find by subtracting your age from 170. To check on your rate while in training, count your pulse for six seconds immediately after running; then add a zero. If your pulse rate is too fast for your age, back up your training a couple of days until the rate is within the measure. If your pulse rate is under, feel free to accelerate the training gradually; but take another check after a few days have passed.

An easy rule of thumb for not exceeding *your* safe rate was passed on to me a few years ago. On my first Pacific visit, I was running on a New Zealand track when a man ran up beside me and tried to start a conversation. Annoyed, I indicated that it was too hard to talk and run at the same time. He asked me to stop a minute. Then he explained that if it was difficult for me to make light conversation while running, then the chances were that I was pushing myself too hard. He explained in detail about the correlation between training rate and age. "If you can't talk, you're sprinting," he said. I didn't pay much attention to that until I learned later that he was the famed track coach Arthur Lydiord. When in doubt now, whether running or climbing, I always have a little conversation with myself and thank him aloud for that advice. So if you see a runner or climber with his lips moving, he may be testing his exertion level in order to keep a consistent heart rate.

Running Style. If you've followed my outline, there is not much chance of your being injured in two weeks of training, regardless of your running form. But there are things you should know as you increase your activity. You need to be conscious of all the elements of running style that, improperly done, might cause you distress when you are out in the wilderness.

How you breathe is important in both climbing and running. It's best to inhale air through the nose and exhale through the mouth. Take air in through the mouth only when it is impossible to get enough through the nose. (If you have small nostrils, it's no crime to inhale through the mouth when under exertion.) Try, before running each day, to breathe using your abdomen. Expand it to take in air and feel it flatten as you exhale. Belly breathing expands the entire oxygen-intake system. Put your hands on your stomach so you can actually feel the expansion and flattening.

I find it helpful to hyperventilate for the first few yards when I start out jogging. Hyperventilating is forced breathing at a faster than normal pace. Skin divers do it to load up their lungs before they exert themselves. It's also helpful when climbing with a pack, especially at high altitudes. However, forced breathing for too long or without physical need can cause dizziness.

You should also know the proper form for running. The heel touches the ground slightly earlier than the ball of the foot (you strike the ground almost flat footed), and then rolls straight forward toward the toe with weight even. Finally the toe pushes off again.

Improper foot placement can lead to ailments of the back, knees, hip joint, and ankles. Correct foot action is automatic for most of us, but if you develop problems, check your shoes to analyze wear. For jogging over two miles a day on streets of concrete, one should have good, straight-ahead running shoes with thick cushions and solid arch supports.

Swing your arms straight ahead in balance with your stride, carrying your forearm just below the elbow. Try to relax your upper body. Tune in to your "body talk"—feel what's happening. If your hands are tense and tight, your shoulders and neck will receive tension later. Carry your shoulders low; relax. It takes a lot of stress off the legs if the upper body moves rhythmically with the lower body. Don't let the lower body carry the upper body; they must function together to become one light, floating unit. Look for, develop and enjoy a rhythm in your running. It should be part of your walking, hiking and climbing too.

Vary your running. Start with some short steps, then stretch and reach for bigger spaces. Let the lower leg swing forward, pendulumlike; then use your feet and toes to grab the ground. Feel your foot "throwing" the ground behind you. (Walk with the same rhythmic stretching—feel the full extension of your limbs, ankle, arch, toe.) Try to run over uneven ground if you are running in daylight. The variety is good for your ankles and feet and conditions your reflexes to the type of terrain you'll find on hikes. Modest hills are good training, but try to avoid steep grades for the training period.

Go slowly! You're training to be a finisher, not a racer. It's survival running. In the beginning, think of your body as an experimental aircraft you're testing. Cruise, throttle, make gentle turns, keep your eyes on the temperature, rpm's, etc. After five days, if there is no "strain to the frame, ping, or motor knock," you can speed up for short distances and test your strength with new exercises.

Self-communing, talking to yourself, and analyzing what you're doing while running helps you to relax and to find your groove for the long haul, as well as helping to fight boredom and to tune you in to body talk. Be patient; training is cumulative.

Take in plenty of liquid before and after each training session. Many joggers run dehydrated, which isn't good. "If your urine isn't clear at least once a day, you're too dehydrated," states Dr. Jack Scaff, the famed Honolulu marathon trainer.

OTHER TRAINING HINTS. If your monthly period occurs during the training, don't break routine unless absolutely necessary. But if you get a cold, stop and cure it. A virus cold inflames the muscles, including the heart (a condition called viral myocarditis). Running worsens it, sometimes causing palpitations and premature ventricular contractions (VCs)—an irregular heartbeat.

Finally, be kind to your feet. Any one of the twenty-six bones in each foot could cause you discomfort. Remove your shoes when possible. Wiggle the feet when sitting; massage them to keep the muscles toned and circulation moving. Elevate them periodically throughout the day. Go barefooted. Walk often in the yard and on the grass, as well as on thick rugs. Trim the nails straight across; allow a space of one inch between toes and shoe interior. Change shoes often during the week; wear flats most of the day.

Running is the best possible training exercise you can do. If for some reason you can't run, try to get the equivalent amount of exercise from one of the sports listed below.

The effectiveness of aerobic exercise can be measured in the amount of fuel—calories—you burn up during the activity. The following chart for the average 152-pound person in activity for one hour measures the calories used and therefore rates that activity. If your weight is less than 152 pounds, you use fewer calories; if more, you burn more. You can raise the level of calories used up by increasing the speed.

(The following figures are from *Executive Fitness Newsletter* published by Rodale Press.)

ACTIVITY	CALORIES/HOUR
Running (7 mph = 8.58 min. each mile)	847
Cross-country skiing (5 mph)	709
Bicycling (13 mph)	651
Jogging (5.5 mph) (a 10-min. mile = 6 mph)	651
Handball—vigorous—single	591
Tennis " "	591
Squash	591
Downhill skiing	585
Swimming (crawl 45 yards/one min.)	529
Canoeing—rowing (4 mph)	429
Walking (4½ mph)	401

Diet While Training

The food you eat during training should be of the same variety as that you'll eat on trips. In this way your body can adjust in advance to getting the best mileage and will not have to suffer a complete change when you begin hiking and climbing. Don't worry about your weight during the training period; it is the efficiency and strength of your body vehicle that will determine how easily you get up and down that mountain. Total body weight is not important; the amount of free-loading fat you're obliged to carry *is* important.

During training, you're tuning up a high-powered machine to cover terrain at high altitudes. The fuel you use must be high octane, not the empty calories of processed junk. No white bread or cakes, potato chips, Cokes, ice cream, crackers or cookies. Refined sugar burns up valuable anti-stress B vitamins in the body system. Eat light, feel light—body talk again. Honey, raw sugar; cereals, bran; fresh fruit, including bananas and oranges; spinach and tomatoes—all are rich in potassium, which will satisfy the craving for sweets.

Get used to eliminating canned goods and frozen foods, for you won't be able to take them in your pack. Eliminate meat, too—you won't want to carry that in your pack either (outside of beef jerky and pemmican). Powdered eggs, milk, chicken and fresh fish are high in protein and are what you'll probably eat on a wilderness trip.

Other hints: in your purse, carry small packages of nuts, raisins or dried fruit for between-meal snacks so you're not tempted to buy from vending machines; drink water when you feel hungry; take vitamin supplements; avoid salt; cut down on portions; and eat slowly, taking small bites and putting your fork down between bites. The kitchen cooking scene is one you'll have to outwit, too, if you want your body to be that high-powered sports vehicle that gets fantastic mileage on a small quantity of fuel.

Days	Warm-up Stretches	Run	Walk	Jog	Strength	Stretch	Sit-up Sets
1	3	/	100yds 4-5x	300yds 4-5x	2	/	1
2	4	/	100yds 5-6x	300yds 5-6x	3	/	1
3	"	/	"	"	"	/	1
4	5	/	100yds 7-8x	300yds 7-8x	4	3	1
5	"	/	"	"	"	"	2
6	6	/	100yds 9-10x	300yds 9-10x	5	5	2
7	"	/	"	"	"	"	2
8	7	/	100yds 11-12x	300yds 11-12x	6	6	2
9	"	/	"	"	"	"	3
10	10	1 mile	100yds 4-5x	300yds 4-5x	7	4	1
11	"	"	"	"	"	"	1
12	9	1½ miles	100yds 2x	300yds 2x	/	8	1
13	"	2 miles	"	"	/	"	1
14	5	2½ miles	100yds 2x	300yds 2x	/	5	1

SUMMARY FOR USE OF TRAINING CHART

Warm-up stretches, before running, should primarily benefit the legs and back. When you feel loose, begin jog-walk. Time yourself the first few days to establish pace—2½ minutes for 300 yards. Check pulse rate—see page 65. After jogging or running, do more stretching and strengthening exercises of your choice. Bent-leg sit-ups are a must.

The training routine will reveal to you a lot about yourself. Be confident that you'll have a great time outdoors *because* you've organized your fourteen-day routine and have dealt with conflicting demands, weather, temperature, and your own body—and stuck out the training period. Hiking and climbing take a tremendous amount of mental energy for the planning, outfitting and organizing before one ever gets off the road.

5 | OUTFITTING

Omit foresight, and you will be complaining before you have begun.
                                        —Leonardo da Vinci

For hiking and climbing, what do you wear, what do you take with you, and what kind of gear do you carry it in? You have to know where you're going before you can answer these questions.

The most important part of "outfitting" is learning how to research and then how to make the right decisions, based on projections and estimates. It takes actual practice and experience to learn that skill.

When studying some of the technical problems of outfitting, keep in mind the basic hiking and climbing categories. There is the ordinary trail hike, which could require as little gear as a summit pack for a one-day excursion—or a larger pack plus sleeping gear and a tent for an overnight excursion. Then there is the ordinary mountain wilderness hike. Finally, there are trail and mountain wilderness expeditions which may call for advanced mountain-climbing gear if you are going for the top. The quantity of gear required for each hike or expedition will also depend on the number in the party, the season and the location.

73

For a summer climb at altitudes of 10,000 feet in the western United States mountain areas, you'll need some winter gear, rain gear, climbing gear, plus stove gear and emergency survival gear. In the winter, add skis, snowshoes and felt boots, plus heavy outerwear.

Getting to the top of the Grand Teton in January is an expedition climb that takes fourteen days. It's an overnight mountain wilderness hike with climbing gear, if made in the summer. A climb in the Himalayas is a two-month expedition costing thousands of dollars and requiring dozens of porters, 50,000 pounds of equipment, and 9,000 items. Colin Fletcher checklisted 138 items without counting food. For a summer's solo hike of seven days, his pack weighed 66½ pounds total, with food and two gallons of water. Minus 17 pounds for water, his total solo summer pack for one week was equal to 49½ pounds. On mountain expeditions you need not carry water, for streams and snows make water available (just take a small canteen). If you're with a group of hikers, two to four people, your load will be less because you will share the use of many items—no duplicate equipment! That's the reason it's best that you pack together or under the direction of the expedition leader.

Technical rock climbing in summer can be for one day or several. You may need special clothes, as for expedition climbing, but you will not require a tent or stove. You will need special hardware carabiners, pitons, nuts, chocks, blocks, stoppers (aluminum wedges made to stop you if you fall), slings, harnesses, hammock, étrier (a nylon loop supported by a nut or piton which fits the foot like a stirrup), and a safety helmet.

Alpine or ice climbing is winter climbing of sheer

hard ice and frozen snow on near-vertical walls and frozen falls. The activity requires special hardware ice axes, ten-point crampons (which strap to your boots so you can climb ice the way a telephone lineman climbs wooden poles), and helmets. Ice climbing is good practice for expedition assaults on snow-covered peaks—but it is an exotic, dangerous day sport in itself.

Winter hiking and climbing requires even more specialized equipment, such as an ice axe, crampons, avalanche cord (a 25-foot cord, attached to the climber, which rises to the top of the snow to help others find her if she's buried), glacier glasses, snow-shoes, and alpine and cross-country skis, plus the usual climbing gear. The safest and least expensive way to begin is with a professionally led group, since they will provide the know-how and equipment. Winter hiking and climbing is not the way to begin your hiking experience. Winter is unforgiving in the wilderness; one can quickly reach the raw edge of survival. It is best to start out in better weather and advance with experts.

The suppliers of climbing equipment can be invaluable in helping you decide what you'll need to take. Even though most manufacturers naturally want all their products sold, the salespeople in climbing shops generally feel a sense of responsibility to the climber. A beginner should invest many hours in shop talk with clerks in these shops and with friends who are climbing enthusiasts about uses and needs before purchasing anything. Guard against the trend to buy brand names, bright colors, or a designer look, fancy attachments, or trimmings. Buy for simple utility and durability. Don't buy new supplies if second-hand ones cost one-half to two-thirds less and are in good condition. Don't buy at all if you can borrow or rent. This adviser makes only one exception—buy your own boots! All other gear and clothing you'll need can be washed, aired, sprayed, cleaned, repaired, and thus used by many without disturbing your sanitary enjoyment. The prospect of second-hand clothing and sleeping bags may go against the basic materialistic fashion syndrome many American women have grown up with, but you'll find it a great relief if you can overcome that fussy habit. No matter how much you spend, there is no way you're going to look "party-sparkling" when you've been on the trail for a week, sleeping on the ground and hiking in the rain. The men you meet outdoors are going to look very scruffy too. If an attraction develops, it'll be based on shared experiences, mutual admiration, and simple availability. For now, take my word that fancy gear and clothes do not make the man or woman in the mountains.

If your life experience hasn't already done so, the one sure thing hiking and climbing will teach you is true economy and practicality, based on realistic utility. You'll learn fast because you'll have to carry yourself and your gear on the only two feet you command.

You must climb mountains on your feet, and all your piety and wit cannot cancel half a yard.

—Brooks Atkinson

Buying Your Boots

Getting your feet fitted properly with boots is the first and most important step, followed almost at once by the training program. Squash any desire to pick out fancy or designer boots, and don't try to squeeze into "neat little numbers." You need lots of interior room for extra socks, foot swelling, comfort, and weight-carrying spread. A boot that is roomy in fit will ventilate better, prevent blisters, and keep the foot drier and warmer than a boot that feels snug when tried on in the store. Your boots need hard toe caps, stiff sides, good arches for support, adjustable laces, tongues designed to be waterproof, and Vibram soles. Most women, including my wife, have a tendency to choose boots that are of flimsy construction because the proper ones feel uncomfortable and stiff. It is only recently that manufacturers of outdoor equipment and boots have begun to take notice of women's special needs. Some are producing boots in smaller men's sizes and/or boots cut on a woman's narrower last. If your foot is narrow or small, ask to see boots cut on a woman's last. An average or wide foot may be content in a shorter men's boot if the sole is not too heavy. There is an adage: "For every pound on your foot, you add two to your back."

You want a boot that will prevent strain or sprain to the ankle, because twenty miles on one foot, with a 40-pound pack, is even more difficult for the climber than for the downhill skier. Up to the point of rock climbing, it can be said that the more difficult the terrain and/or the heavier the pack, the more support you need on your feet. Since you probably can't afford to buy a different boot for trail hikes, light backpacking, day hiking, climbing expeditions, etc., you should get one that is heavy duty but has a sole that bends. Unbending climbing boots or "sneakers with Vibram soles" are for special climbing projects.

Like the skier's, good climber's boots will probably cost $50 to $125 for acceptable quality. I recommend that women hikers and climbers, even though only beginning, be prepared to buy the best boots—$75 to $100. Remember, you've saved $20 to $30 by not buying a fancy jogging or warm-up suit. That should make it easier to spend more for hiking boots if you need to. Don't shop for boots by price, however. Look for the features I've outlined. If you are eighteen to twenty-five, have been a competitive athlete all your life, and feel that you have strong feet and tough skin, you might want to try getting by with a lower quality boot for the first year—until you can get more oriented to the types of outdoor experience. There is the chance you might want to specialize. After you've done your basic hiking and climbing, you may decide, for example, that technical rock climbing is the only outdoor activity you want to continue. The best hiking shoes won't be much help to you for technical rock climbing, and you'll have to get lighter rock climbers anyway. However, my contention is that if you are full-grown adult size when you get boots, even if you do eventually take up some type of specialty climbing, such as rock or ice, that requires another pair of boots, the day will come when you'll need heavy-duty hikers for backpacking into a remote rock area. Good boots, if cared for and used no more than half a dozen times a year, will last a lifetime.

Steve Komito, the best bootmaker I know, divides boot use into four groups:

1. TRAIL HIKING AND MODERATE ROCK CLIMBING: The soles are flexible. Uppers are light and too thin for wet conditions.

2. GENERAL HIKING AND MOUNTAINEERING: Rigid uppers and soles, thick enough for rough terrain and wet conditions, but, if they're good quality, not so stiff and heavy as to become a burden over long distances.

3. TECHNICAL ROCK CLIMBING: The soles may be either flexible or rigid. The uppers are light and thin and poorly suited for extended walking or wet conditions. Unfortunately, the wearer occasionally encounters both.

4. TECHNICAL MOUNTAINEERING: Uppers and soles are thick and rigid. Walking comfort is of secondary importance (at least to the manufacturers). Cold-weather mountaineering boots may have either flexible or rigid soles. Uppers are waterproof, and there may be a removable inner boot.

The boot you need is the general hiking and mountaineering boot described in category 2, above. Avoid window shopping in the other categories.

Steve thinks the best boot may be the "New World." It is one he helped design. It has a big-toe military last that creates a L'il Abner look, but Steve feels the fit justifies the look. No stitching shows; in fact, it has complete inner construction. The major top seams are sunk into grooves to protect the threads from damage. The lining leather does not come out over the top of the boot; thus, there is no wear on this soft leather and no replacement is necessary. The heel lining is made from the same leather as the sole, so it is tough and wear-resistant. The lacing starts above the toe joint, and the boot is fastened inside.

Komito also likes the Pivetta model No. 8 from Italy. It is one of the few boots with full-grained leather uppers. The boot is inside-fastened, which provides greater durability. However, it is sometimes too narrow in the toe and too loose in the heel. Steve rates it "C" for fit and "A" for strength and durability. This boot comes in five widths and is priced at $80 at the moment.

One of the finest boots is the Kufstein, at $125. It is used by park rangers and trail crews who must get heavy use from their boots over several seasons. It will last through many resolings. The lacing ends up on the arch behind the ball of the foot, and it has a wide toe.

Komito imports a new line of Italian boots because the manufacturer is receptive to his ideas. The Volkswagen boot, as he calls the Allegro, is pure simplicity: clean, light and cheap at $65. No cute accessory touches; no padded ankles. However, there is some padding in the tongue to prevent the foot from slipping forward on downhill trails. (Thick socks help, too.)

The other Italian model is called the Yukon, and it comes in five widths. It has an improved padded tongue and an inside scree collar that gives closeness of fit without structural weakness or exposure to abrasion. This model sells for $80 at the time of this writing.

Komito will send a catalogue on request. Write to:

Komito Boots
P.O. Box 2106
Estes Park, Colorado 80517

Steve Komito has devised a method for measuring your foot on paper so that you can order by mail. But please remember that it takes time to order, and it's expensive to return the boots if you're not satisfied with the fit.

Fitting boots can be very difficult and time consuming. It is essential that you find a store that carries a good inventory of sizes and styles. You will need sturdy construction, but since a woman's feet are smaller, there's no need to have the weight or thickness of men's soles. Some hiking-shoe companies make the same sole thickness on all sizes. If you weigh only 115 pounds, you don't need soles designed for a 200-pound man. You'll need to determine whether the sole will bend or "give" in a forward direction as you walk. If the boot sole is artificially stiff, it isn't good for hiking. There should be a little give in the sole even when the boot is new.

When you try on boots, wear one pair of heavy rag wool socks. Once you have the boots tightly laced, you should be able to kick a wood beam or concrete wall hard without any pain to your toes. That is the test for "no slip" on the downhill trail, where you might otherwise blister the toe ends. You should allow extra room for normal foot swelling from walking, plus room for another pair of heavy rag wool socks. The extra warmth may be needed.

Check toe space by unlacing the boot and pushing your toes, with one pair of socks on, all the way forward. While standing, bend your knees forward; you should be able to insert a finger between your heel and the back of the boot without exerting any pressure.

Avoid those stores with sales personnel who sell boots to students for wear on the street or in the classroom. These clerks don't know how to fit correctly for hiking and climbing.

Breaking in Your Boots

Here is the Paul Petzoldt method of breaking in a boot for a comfortable fit in the shortest amount of time: Fill the boots with water to ankle height, and allow them to stand for a few minutes so that the water can soak into the interior of the leather. Then pour off the water. Wearing one pair of socks, or with the boots laced up tightly, walk for at least half an hour. Wear the boots for a couple more hours to allow them to conform to your foot shape. It won't damage the boot to be damp. Avoid drying boots by any special method. Wet and wear again, this time with two pairs of socks if damp feet bother you. Once again, avoid drying boots in the sun or by a fire. More damage is done to boots from drying than from dampness. Later, when the fit feels right to you, the inside leather can be treated with a preservative.

Other Equipment

After you have acquired your boots, consider buying a so-called man's watch (because of its size), one with a luminous dial, which will give you comfort on long nights in your sleeping bag. The watch will also be an aid in timing yourself during the training period. One with a second hand will help you rate your heartbeat. One that's waterproof or water-resistant is desirable in case of accident or rain. A cloth band is more suitable for extreme cold and temperature changes than leather or metal. Carry a spare strap—they're light. Timex makes some watches of this type that were selling for $15.20 at the time of this writing. If you can afford the battery-operated model, it is self-winding.

You will want and need a summit pack, so named because it was originally invented to carry a few needed items on that final one-day climb to the summit and back to camp. These are generally made of nylon or treated canvas. They are useful for training and short day trips, as well as for general usage around town or on the campus. There are many makes with similar designs. My only recommendation is that you purchase one having a large storage area in the basic cavity and some separate outside pockets. A pack that folds small when empty, is highly durable, and has adjustable shoulder straps is best.

As for clothing, you may need to buy a couple of pairs of heavy rag wool socks—new. The rest you can rescue from your family attic or pick up at Salvation Army or army surplus stores. There are a few other supplies you may need to buy new: a metal soap dish with lid; a metal toothbrush container; some plastic bags or stuff sacks; some skin oil; insect repellent; and food. Save most of your money for air fare or bus fare.

The following are checklists that should be studied and considered when making plans, but please don't think you must take everything listed on each trip. The less you take, the better. I have purposely omitted lists and discussions pertaining to backpack frames, tents, sleeping bags, stoves, etc., since I suggest that you refrain from buying these items until you've had extended experience in the outdoors. You can probably borrow or rent equipment from members of the group you're going with or from local retailers they might recommend. See the Appendix for places to go for equipment.

Outfitting Checklist

CLOTHING

Halter or bikini tops—Instead of brassieres.

T-shirts—Cotton

Underpants—Cotton—a fancy nylon pair only if it perks your morale.

Wool long Johns—Avoid all synthetics under clothing.

Sweaters—Wool; only long-sleeved pullovers—crew neck. One lightweight, one heavy and long to cover hips—sew on length from reject sweater.

Walking shorts—Cotton or corduroy—you can cut off jeans.

Long pants—Farmer's overalls are good for climbing, as are loose-fitting jeans with baggy knees. Men's pants are best for female climbers. Steal your brother's or friend's pants, sew on heavy extra seat and knee patches, and insert string ties at ankles for the best hiking and climbing pants ever. If you attach (red) suspenders by sewing them with heavy thread, you can have "loose drawers" without fear of losing your pants. Use wool pants for summer expeditions in northern areas.

Belt—Leather—needed to attach things to for carrying. Get extra length to fit over winter clothing.

Socks—Wool only—knee length and ankle length.

Fiberfill jacket and pants—Dacron 99 Fiberfill dries quickly, like wool; down does not.

Rain poncho—Take two. Make sure one is large enough to fit over pack.

Rain pants

Wool shirt—Nehru-type collar, no lining, no zipper. Large enough to fit over sweaters.

Gloves—Wool mittens for warmth inside windbreaker mittens; leather for handling rope.

Hats—Wool stocking cap that covers your ears; felt fedora with chin string attached for sun.

Bandannas—Several large ones to tie up hair and to keep dust away from neck.

Swimsuit—Optional—you can swim without it.

Moccasins

Winter clothing

Windproof parka—Large enough to fit over bulky sweater.

Wind pants

Wool pants

Wool shirt

Combination wool hat and face mask

Long Johns—Cotton or wool.

Down vest

Down jacket

Wet gear—New materials (such as Gortex and Bukflex) have been developed that are 100 percent waterproof, yet "breathe." Their durability is as yet unproven; wait until you're into serious climbing to investigate.

Gaiters—To cover ankles or up to knees. They seal off boot tops from snow and dirt.

Expedition mitts—Down or Fiberfill; should be tied together with cord.

Overmitts—Must be wind- and waterproof.

PERSONAL SUPPLIES

Toothbrush

Toothpaste—Very small amount.

Soap—Biodegradable.

Comb—Metal.

Fingernail file—Metal—emery boards disintegrate when wet or crushed.

Towel—Small.

Lip and nose protection—For above 10,000 feet.

Insect repellent—Cutters.

Suntan lotion—Small plastic container.

Face cream—Cleansing or moisturizing important in dry air. Use small plastic container, e.g., Nivea.

Hand lotion

Glacier cream—Necessary in snowy areas at altitudes above 10,000 feet to prevent ultraviolet rays from burning your skin.

Toilet paper—Two small rolls with rubber bands to hold them. Store separately in plastic bags.

Watch—Waterproof, with woven nylon strap.

Sanitary napkins or tampons—With paper, not plastic, inserters.

Needle with thread and extra string—Nylon.

Tape

Moleskin

Salt pills

Laxative—Herbal type.

Canteen—You may want your own small plastic container for drinking water. Buy two at the same time; if one breaks or leaks, you'll have an extra lid. Besides, you can use the second one for some other liquid, such as cooking oil.

Waterproof container for wooden matches—keep sewing needle there, too.

Whistle—Loud police type.

Eyeglasses—Take an extra pair and a string attachment.

Contact lenses—Take an extra pair. Carry both in small case on nylon cord around your neck.

Flashlight—Lightweight. Also take bulbs and batteries. Penlite with extra Mallory batteries—alkaline AA size. Put tape over switch to prevent their being turned on accidentally.

Headlamp—Lightweight, for night climbing or reading. Also take spare batteries and bulbs.

Candles—1 to 2 inches thick, no more than 4 inches long. Take two.

Sunglasses

Camera—Also accessories and film.

Snow-goggles—For protection at high altitude from wind and glare.

Binoculars

Compass

Writing and reading material

Maps and guidebooks; notes of route advice

Pocketknife—Swiss army or Boy Scout type.

Waterproofing boot sealer

Rubbing alcohol

Foot powder

FIRE KIT

Matches and shavings in waterproof container

Cigarette lighter

Flint

Stove

Fuel for stove

BASIC EQUIPMENT

Sleeping bag and stuff sack

Sleeping pad

Tent (Warmlite), poles and pegs

Ground sheet (air mattress)

Nylon cord

Stuff bags—Three to five of assorted sizes and colors, all with drawstring clamps. Good for keeping gear dry and in order.

Plastic bags—Heavy-duty bags in various sizes; zip-lock for film, books, small items.

Accessory straps or cords to strap gear to outside of pack.

Expedition framepack

Large rucksack

Summit pack

FOOD

Powdered nonfat milk

Fruit drink mix—Tang, Wyler's lemonade with vitamin C.

Margarine—Comes in liquid form.

Peanut butter

Energy bars

Chocolate

Grains

Cornmeal

Rice

Pasta

Biscuit mix

Dried fruit—Raisins, apricots, apples, etc.

Salt

Salt tablets

Tea bags

Coffee

Cocoa

Sugar

Herbs and spices—Garlic powder, curry powder, parsley flakes, dry mustard, oregano, cinnamon, nutmeg.

Dehydrated mixed vegetables

Dehydrated potatoes

Packages of dehydrated soup

Packages of dehydrated instant gravy

Packages of dehydrated beans

Packages of dehydrated fruit

Beef jerky

Meat bars

Cereals—granola, wheat germ, oats, etc.

Mixed nuts without salt

Honey

Puddings

Condiments

Rock salt

Dry yeast

Vinegar and oil—Lemon juice instead of vinegar if you prefer.

Pemmican—When outfitting for any extended trip involving cold weather, I suggest using the following recipe to prepare pemmican:

   Slice beef or other red meat thin. Cut into narrow strips an inch wide by eight inches long. Sundry ("jerky") for two or three days (a clothesline will do;

dry weather is a must). Smoke a day or two by hanging on racks over a low fire, keeping the heat and smoke in with a covering tarp (an oven at low temperature will also do). Then crumble the meat, mix with an equal quantity of rendered fat, and seal in waterproof bags. It should keep in that form for up to a year. Mix in raisins or dried berries to improve flavor and nutritional value. The Chippewas of northern Wisconsin and Minnesota used maple sugar.

Pemmican is a complete food, with or without the berries. For an average-sized woman, two pounds per day is enough.

COOKING GEAR

Stove	Matches
2 pots	Plastic scrubber
1 frypan	Plastic bags
Cup	Biodegradable soap
Fork and spoon	Can opener
Wooden bowl	Plastic water jug

FIRST-AID KIT

2 compresses	1 plastic tube pain pills
1 roll gauze	1 plastic tube Halazone tablets
1 roll tape	1 tube sunscreen ointment
Ace bandages	Butterfly Band-Aids

6 | FIRST EXPEDITION

Life is not breath but action, the use of our senses, mind, faculties, every part of ourselves which makes us conscious of our being.

—Jean Jacques Rousseau

It's impossible to learn all you need to know to go on a hiking or climbing expedition simply from books. Therefore, you have two choices: Accompany a boy or girlfriend who is not a beginner; or attend a hiking or climbing school that has a professional expert as leader-instructor. I recommend that you begin with a professional expert.

Following are four major advantages of going with a professional school.

First: In a pro-led school group, you will be with other beginners who will identify, adapt and feel in a way that will express a very special togetherness. It's an experience you should undergo firsthand. Meeting and sharing with strangers in a new environment is something you will remember for a long time, and having an expert guide to handle the critical decisions will eliminate the trouble areas.

Second: You will be taught outdoor living skills and rules of conservation in an organized and rational way that will eliminate complications and confusion.

Third: You will learn the techniques of rock climbing, use of ropes, etc.—highly technical skills that must be mastered to ensure the safety of you and future climbing friends.

Fourth: If you choose a school or organized group for your initial trip, most of the special equipment will either be supplied to you or rented to you inexpensively; a friend may or may not have that equipment, and you may be unaware of what you're missing until you're on the trail—too late.

Starting out with a friend or friends on the beginning experience has certain features that can complicate and confuse the learning period. Certainly the fact that mutual trust and respect have already been established in your former relationships will make you less likely to be anxious or nervous, as might be the case with strangers. As a beginner who has doubts and reservations, you may regard that as a plus. I don't. I believe you *should* undergo the pressures of trying to measure up in a group of strangers who are also beginners at hiking and climbing and outdoor living. In technical rock climbing particularly, learning with a friend you admire and love may have the advantage of giving you confidence and trust to take what may seem to you to be unnecessary risks, for you know that you will be cared for and loved. When Dad put each of us in the saddle at age three, we didn't tremble as we did three years later on our first day in kindergarten with a strange teacher and classmates. On the other hand, how can you know how expert your boy or girlfriend is at technical rock climbing? If you planned to take flying lessons from a friend, at least you would know whether he or she was licensed to fly solo or as an instructor. It's just part of flying language to talk of one's license qualification. "I have a private license with twenty hours' solo time" or "I've got my twin engine rating and am working on my instructor's ticket." Climbers are neither licensed nor rated. You could be putting a lot of misplaced trust in someone who is not qualified to be on rock with a beginner, let alone to teach. I believe it is better to struggle within yourself to overcome exaggerated fear (and to win) than to depend on faith in a loved one to keep you from harm.

Also, going with friends more experienced than you places you in a dependent position. Shyness may prevent your questioning or contradicting a decision. If you're with a boy friend and you're the beginner, the usual course is to follow like a squaw and just help with the chores without entering into any decisions. He will satisfy his ego by playing the role of "chief," but you'll be dissatisfied because you won't learn or enjoy much.

As I stated earlier in this chapter, it is best to begin your outdoor training accompanied by an expert and go with the boy friend *only* after you have acquired some outdoor knowledge and skill. Then work out in advance some kind of sharing that will satisfy you. The boy friend may be more experienced in certain areas, but shy in others. Let him know you want to discuss and share leadership, navigation, cooking, campsite decisions, etc., as you go. Work out such items as costs, equipment, checklists and duties, and insist on paying 50 percent of the expenses. An outdoor experience shared intimately with a beloved friend can be great fun even though you are inexperienced, but don't expect it to be the best learning experience. More than one week of wilderness hiking with a boy friend is certainly a good test of compatibility and could be one of life's most romantic adventures—and I don't mean sexually. There is a misconception among younger people that if boys and girls go into the woods together, it implies orgies and free love. Many parents also have that impression and thereby hold back young daughters and even sons from what are probably the most healthy co-ed social experiences they could have at that age. You'll find that after you and a strange man spend 8 to 14 daylight hours carrying backpacks that weigh from 40 to 70 pounds through dense forests and over rugged boulder-strewn inclined terrain; and feeding your hungry faces by cooking over primitive fires or simple stoves, neither one of you will be very interested in amorous adventures, no matter how attractive he may have seemed on that first day or how oversexed he sounded by his earlier comments. By the time you have put up a tent, arranged sleeping bags, and handled the night fire and other chores, you'll look at his hands and yours and at his scruffy whiskered face, feel the bark and crumbs in your hair, rub the sore muscles of your back, thighs and feet, and you will be thinking of only one thing: how soon you can get into your sleeping bag *alone!* Because he has also looked at *you* and because he too is exhausted, his thoughts will also be on sleep. This might not apply to leisurely canoe trips downstream or horsepacking trips with wranglers to handle horses and cooking chores; but the hiking experience—in a new environment and carrying your own gear—is so absorbing that the atmosphere—despite the beauty of nature and the mood; despite the night and the crackling fire—does not encourage sex.

One must master the basic skills of hiking, backpacking, camping and survival in extremes of weather to get near the summits; then one must be skilled in technical rock, snow and ice climbing to reach the peak. Traditionally one learns the technical skills in the second phase. I believe it makes no difference if one reverses the procedure by starting with a few days of technical climbing; it might be the stimulus to spur you on. However, it's important to realize that you're not ready for an expedition just because you've had some technical rock or ice climbing. In fact, I would guess that Hillary never did any technical rock or ice climbing before conquering Mount Everest—and I know Tenzing Norgay didn't. Be assured, however, that they had done lots of hiking and outdoor living at high altitude in cold temperatures.

In the Appendix I've compiled a list of schools that provide instructors for trips of ten days or more. To find others that might be closer to the area you're interested in visiting, call the local YMCA, sporting goods stores, Chamber of Commerce, colleges, or some of the climbing clubs or organizations listed in the Appendix.

Two of the best organizations to go to in order to learn the beginning basics of hiking and climbing are Colorado Outward Bound and the National Outdoor Leadership School (NOLS).

Outward Bound originated during the Second World War, its purpose being to help British sailors develop the "spiritual tenacity" and will to survive shipwrecks. Since it came to this country in 1962, it has quickly evolved from sea survival to include hiking and climbing and wilderness experience for people of all ages throughout the United States and in many foreign countries. There are special courses for "women only" and "men only," as well as many co-ed courses of different degrees of hardship and length in all seasons. Its main thrust, in addition to the teaching of basic outdoor skills, is on personal development and self-discovery. The original letterhead motto "To serve, to strive, and not to yield" and the more recent "I have learned that there are no limits to my efforts, unless I limit myself" together convey the philosophies of testing, proving, decision making, confidence building, etc. All special equipment except boots and clothing is supplied.

NOLS was started in 1965 by Paul Petzoldt, who developed the original mountaineering courses for Colorado Outward Bound. NOLS courses are offered primarily in Wyoming and other western areas, but do include expeditions to Africa, Alaska, Baja and Mexico. Two special climbing courses for advanced students are a climb of Mount McKinley in Alaska and a winter climb of the Grand Teton. All courses are co-ed, including one for older adults called "The 39ers," for which the true age minimum is about thirty. Additional courses have age minimums beginning at sixteen, eighteen and twenty-one. All equipment, including clothing, is supplied. Boots can be rented or purchased in Lander, Wyoming, when you arrive for outfitting.

The main thrust of NOLS is not the same as that of Outward Bound. There is not as much emphasis on survival, physical hardship, testing and proving. Rather, NOLS emphasizes conservation and the enjoyment of wilderness experiences. Both are non-profit organizations. Outward Bound is able to charge slightly less, probably because it is older and larger and receives more financial contributions. My sons, daughters, wife and I have all been a part of or monitored several courses at both organizations. Both teach basic skills excellently. NOLS certainly has more to offer the advanced student. I believe that all women interested in hiking and climbing should take a basic summer co-ed course of fourteen days or more—one that includes mountaineering instructions—at either Outward Bound or NOLS, whichever suits their time schedule best. I have listed other schools that may have courses equally good for beginner hiking and climbing experiences. The *New York Times* estimates that there are at least 3,000 schools and organizations with courses in outdoor "action-oriented learning."

After your "basic," to use an old army expression, the opportunities for short outdoor classes and exotic expedition climbs in foreign countries are limitless. A growing number of women's organizations and travel companies offer particularly appealing programs.

One—Women in the Wilderness—started in 1976 as a nonprofit educational organization staffed with volunteers and grew from 6 to 5,000 paying members in one year. The group has already established a national network through newsletters and monthly program series. Trips to date have all been led by women, but male members are accepted, I'm happy to report.

From their bulletin in the fall of 1977:

We feel that the heart of our work lies in supporting women becoming the leaders of their own lives. Participation in the world out-of-doors is a direct way for us as women to experience our competence and challenge our sense of adventure.

They say the organization was

. . . designed to promote trips, expeditions, outings and educational experiences led by women in the out-of-doors. We

*support opportunities for women to hold leadership positions,
receive training and find work in outdoor programs based on
the assumption that the wilderness is a radical learning environment for women today. The wilderness furnishes us
with opportunities to develop new role models for women by
seeing each other as competent, adventuresome and willing
to take risks. For some, a walk in San Francisco's Golden
Gate Park will be a challenge; for others it will be climbing
in Nepal. All levels of participation in outdoor activities are
equally valid. We are open to men and only stipulate that any
trip listed in our calendar be led by a woman. We see ourselves as an inclusive rather than exclusive organization
which benefits men as well as women.*

Their stories and artwork in their bulletin are so
well done that I believe the $6 membership fee is
more than justified. Sample stories from the Fall 1977
issue are "The American Women's Himalayan Expedition 1978: A Vision"; "Climbing Aconcagua," a
poem; "Conversation with Margo St. James: Growing
Up Wild"; "The Outdoor Woman: Clothing and
Equipment Surveyed"; "Environmental News—The
Frisco Bay Messel Group"; "Drawings—From the
Natural World"; "Edible Plants—The Cattail"; and
"Coming Out—Fall Trips and Outings, in the Bay
and Around the Country."

Then, for your ultimate exotic climb of Mount
Everest, Mount Kilimanjaro, the Baltoro Glacier, the
volcanoes of Mexico or Hawaii, the Cordillera Blanc,
the mountains of Bolivia, the Peruvian Andes, or the
north Alps of Japan; for a hike along the Annapurna
range in Nepal on the Lhotse Glacier, Hongu/
Everest/Cho Oyu, or the Rolwaling Himalaya; or even
for your first conquest of an unclimbed rock-ice peak
(in 1978 it would have been Kishtwar Himalaya at
21,000 feet, Mount McKinley or Mount Sanford in

Alaska, or the High Arctic to the North Pole), there is Mountain Travel, a company based in Albany, California, founded in 1967 by Leo Le Bon, a Belgian explorer-businessman, and a group of world-renowned climber-explorers. This company and dozens of others that have recently been formed organize, guide, supply and lead climbs and hikes on foreign mountain expeditions all over the world. They have removed the hardships pertaining to language, money exchange, barter, etc., present in the days of Stanley and Livingstone by acting as organizer and outfitter.

The Mountain Travel leadership roster reads like the Who's Who of climbing:

Tenzing Norgay — the Sherpa who first climbed Mount Everest with Sir Edmund Hillary in 1953.

Lute Jerstad — another of the first five Americans to scale Mount Everest on the historic 1963 expedition; he led the first ascent of a Mountain Travel group (1977) up the unclimbed Bethartali (21,000 feet) in the Garhwal Himalayas.

Kurt Diemberger — a top climber; the only living climber with two first ascents of 8,000-meter peaks to his credit; author of *Summits and Secrets*.

John Cleare — British photographer and mountaineer, with several books of mountain pictures on the stands.

John Fischer — director of the Palisade School of Mountaineering; he guides the Ecuador climb.

Jan Tiura — a woman — leads a Hawaiian climb and the Trans-Siberian climb.

Linda Liscom — another woman — leads the Bhutan and Darjeeling climbs, as well as climbs in the Peruvian Highlands.

Arlene Blum, the leader of the first American all-woman climb of Annapurna, did some of her early climbing abroad with Mountain Travel. Le Bon says that his group has taken literally hundreds of "female climbers" over sixty years of age to high altitude without a fatality. These women, however, most of whom have grown up climbing in the western Sierra Nevada range as lifelong members of the Sierra Club, are direct descendants of John Muir's wilderness philosophy. Judy Chaffen, a seventy-six-year-old woman now living in a retirement home in San Francisco, went on a Nepal trek at an altitude of 18,000 feet last year. In 1963 she took a Sierra Club hiking trip to South America with Le Bon. And in 1967 she was among those on Mountain Travel's first Nepal trip, which included Little Tukche Peak, at 20,000 feet. By his calculations, 100 trips a year with approximately 10 people a trip equals 1,000 men and women, or approximately 500 women on adventure expeditions in strange countries.

See the Appendix on page 257 for a list of places to check out for instruction and page 263 for expeditions.

7 | ON THE TRAIL

I only went out for a walk
But finally concluded to stay out till sundown.
For going out, I found, was really going in!
—John Muir

A woman contemplating her first hike or climb with experienced friends or with a professionally led group of strangers should make it her business to educate herself in advance with some basic facts about the area to be explored. If you have never hiked or camped out overnight, the experience will be totally foreign. In case, for any reason, you should become separated from your group, you ought to have the information that would prepare you for survival alone.

Before your group departs for the mountains, look at a road map with your leader or a local sheriff or ranger who knows the area. He or she can help you mark the general route you will take off the road to your final destination. He or she can also indicate the towns and help you estimate the distance from your route to these towns. Since even a two-week trip will cover a small area on a road map, you can easily cut out that section of the map and tape it inside a small blank notebook that will serve as a diary of your trip.

Put the notebook and a couple of three- or four-inch wooden pencils into a plastic bag with a compass. Also pack a single-edge razor blade taped to cardboard, and a metal fingernail file—both are useful for many tasks, including sharpening pencils. You can carry this small package in your jacket, pants or shirt pocket. Assuming that you can find direction with the compass and read the map, you'll always be able to walk to a road or town. Some people have more trouble than others finding directions—i.e., which way is true north? You should mark north, south, east and west in large letters on the edges of your simple road map section. Then when you go to climb a mountain, mark which direction your route takes and mentally note the pattern of the sun as it moves east to west. I will bet that by the end of the trip that plastic bag and map will be at the bottom of your pack.

You'll also need to know about the local weather in the area of your expedition. That knowledge will help you decide on the proper clothing to bring. Just call the Weather Bureau; or, better still, make a personal visit if you can. You'll learn more by presenting your fresh face to people with routine jobs who welcome a friendly break. Ask the average nighttime and daytime temperatures; ask about the coldest and warmest temperatures ever recorded. Check the average wind velocity and the maximum velocity, for you need to consider the wind chill factor when deciding upon clothes. Wind chill means that cold weather is colder when there is wind. A temperature that registers just below freezing can have the effect of forty below if it is combined with high wind. Following is a chart so that.you can calculate wind chill.

Ask about rain and snow patterns and the frequency of storms. Obviously, as a beginner, you can't possibly have the knowledge to make final decisions about gear, clothing and shelter needs. Do that with your leaders and ask them to verbalize their reasoning. It is just as bad to overload your pack with clothing and gear for the worst possible weather as to take too little.

Remembering that altitude in the mountains makes its own weather, and that the temperature decreases three degrees for every 1,000 feet you rise, take enough clothes to survive an average night without any other shelter!

You should also know the time-plan for your expedition. How many days to the top? How many miles a day between campsites? Only a ranger or leader who has been over the route has the knowledge of the terrain to provide this kind of information.

WIND CHILL TABLE
AIR TEMPERATURE (°F)

WIND SPEED MPH	35	30	25	20	15	10	5	0	−5	−10	−15	−20	−25	−30	−35	−40	−45
WIND CHILL INDEX (EQUIVALENT TEMPERATURE) · Equivalent in cooling power on exposed flesh																	
4	35	30	25	20	15	10	5	0	−5	−10	−15	−20	−25	−30	−35	−40	−45
5	32	27	22	16	11	6	0	−5	−10	−15	−21	−26	−31	−36	−42	−47	−52
10	22	16	10	3	−3	−9	−15	−22	−27	−34	−40	−46	−52	−58	−64	−71	−77
15	16	9	2	−5	−11	−18	−25	−31	−38	−45	−51	−58	−65	−72	−78	−85	−92
20	12	4	−3	−10	−17	−24	−31	−39	−46	−53	−60	−67	−74	−81	−88	−95	−103
25	8	1	−7	−15	−22	−29	−36	−44	−51	−59	−66	−74	−81	−88	−96	−103	−110
30	6	−2	−10	−18	−25	−33	−41	−49	−56	−64	−71	−79	−86	−93	−101	−109	−116
35	4	−4	−12	−20	−27	−35	−43	−52	−58	−67	−74	−82	−89	−97	−105	−113	−120
40	3	−5	−13	−21	−29	−37	−45	−53	−60	−69	−76	−84	−92	−100	−107	−115	−123
45	2	−6	−14	−22	−30	−38	−46	−54	−62	−70	−78	−85	−93	−102	−109	−117	−125

(Overlaid zone labels: COLD, VERY COLD, BITTER COLD, EXTREME COLD)

WIND SPEEDS GREATER THAN 40 MPH HAVE LITTLE ADDITIONAL CHILLING EFFECT

Topographical maps are helpful, but it takes field experience to understand what one is reading. (See pages 144–46.) If you're an average-size woman, about five feet five, the fastest you could walk over flat ground all day would probably be about three miles an hour. I would guess you'd average twenty miles a day without pack at the elevation of your hometown. If you are carrying a pack and traveling over rough terrain—that is, crossing rocks, stumps and roots on a winding and elevated trail—one mile an hour could be very good progress. Going back downhill either in an emergency or with very strong motivation—like the anticipation of taking a hot bath after two weeks outdoors—you could set a record.

Your leader will have to divide tents, cooking equipment and food among the group. She'll make a guess as to who can carry the most; later, the load division may have to change to keep stragglers from lagging too far behind. Packing a pack is as individual as rock music, but a few basic principles will help minimize the drain on a person's physical reserve. Framepacks come in small, medium and large. Be sure you have help in picking the right size for you. The waistband has a back band that should rest on the upper portion of the buttocks. Most of the weight is carried on the hips. If her pack is fitted properly, a hiker will be able to redistribute weight from hip to shoulders by tightening or loosening the belt. On an easy trail, put heavy items at the top of the pack; on a rough trail, put heavy items low and toward the center of the pack, next to your back. Smaller items in stuff sacks of different colors are generally best put into pockets for easy access. Need I mention that a water bottle and toilet paper in a double plastic bag should be in an accessible pocket?

Before you leave town, make sure the ranger (if you are in a national park) or the sheriff's office, *as well as* someone back home, knows that your group will be in a certain area on a specified route for a specified number of days with a leader whose address you have supplied. Give your parents or husband the name and number of the sheriff or ranger to call if they haven't heard from you three days after your planned return.

Now, after you've waved goodbye to the back of a fast-departing truck or bus, you turn around, look up at the steep trail and mountaintop above you, and you know the moment of truth has arrived. You have trained, you've done your research and homework, you've packed and called home, but have you figured out how to get a 40- to 60-pound pack onto your back? If you were clever, before going to bed in your motel the night before on the last clean white sheets you'll see for a while, you took the time to practice putting that pack onto your back. So today at the trail head in front of these other amateur adventurers you'll look and feel very confident. No movement you'll make under watchful eyes these next days will seem as awkward as getting that pack onto your back the first time. But the main reason for a little technique practice in advance is to learn to save energy. On the frequent rest stops you'll want to stretch and loosen up, and always there is the pack to hoist again.

The easiest method is to place the pack on a log or boulder, which will serve as a loading platform, and slip your arms through the shoulder straps. However, you cannot always count on having a convenient platform.

The easiest way to hoist the heaviest loads is to position the pack upright on the ground, turn your back to it, and slip your arms through the shoulder straps. After you have tightened the straps, lean forward onto your hands and one knee with the pack on your back, stand up with an elegant flair, fasten the waistband—and you're off.

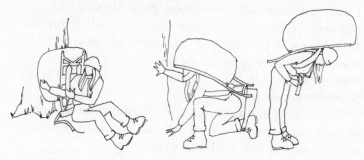

The method most used: With the frame facing you, swing the pack so that the bottom rests on the upper thigh of one leg. While balancing it there, slip the arm on the same side through the loosened shoulder straps. Then, in one motion, swing the pack around your shoulder and onto your back so that you can slip your other arm into its loosened straps. The reverse of this method is also the most common way to unload a pack.

If you are given a big load, don't push yourself to exhaustion. Fatigue causes accidents. You might not want to complain on the first day, but conserve your body's energy and see how you make out on the second and third days. Feel no embarrassment if you are the slowest of the group the first few days; your leader will make adjustments in pack division as he or she sees fit. You should take it on yourself from the first day on to be sure you carry a supply of accessible trail food with you to eat between meals. Have some nuts, granola, M&M's, chocolate candy or dried fruit to nibble on as you go.

You won't have any basis for judging your strength or endurance or even your adaptation to altitude yet, so start slow if you feel any strain.

Your leader will no doubt give you a position in line

on the trail and suggest a spacing distance, usually 6 to 10 feet. Now you're off; but unlike a horseback rider, you won't have the luxury of looking around to enjoy sights while "Old Paint" picks his way up the trail. On most climbing expeditions, even at the trail head the path will be so uneven you'll have to sight-glance almost every step to avoid twisting an ankle. At first you'll have to do most of your looking during the frequent rest stops. As you get practiced, you'll notice stretches ahead that are smooth enough to allow you to look around as you walk—you'll soon be recording your progress with your subconscious mind's eye. From time to time, walk a smooth section backwards (even uphill) to release tension on different muscles and to study the terrain you've covered. It will help you later to remember where you are on the way down, and it will relieve the monotony of plodding in silence.

Every woman should develop her own style of rhythmic walking to save herself from early fatigue. Hands should be swinging on sync, symmetrically and balanced, and should be free to brush aside branches and give support on rocks or trees. Coordinating rhythmic breathing with rhythmic walking will considerably reduce body strain over a period of hours. The number of steps will vary, depending on the steepness of incline, but the breathing should remain the same. When you change gears to smaller steps to go uphill, your heart rate should stay the same. The idea is not to strain your motor by increasing breathing and heart rate to keep up the same pace, but rather to adjust your pace—i.e., take shorter steps—in order to keep breathing and heart rate the same.

If you learn this method in the first few days, you will find that later at higher altitudes you will fare much better than others. You'll arrive at camp with enough reserve energy to help with tent-pitching and cooking without a long rest. And since you won't overheat on the trail you won't need to remove clothing to avoid sweating (to remove clothing, you must remove and then replace the pack, which requires a lot of energy).

The expedition leader will consider the slowest member when setting the pace and arranging rest stops. Stops will be short so that you do not cool off too much, but there should be time for kidney relief, a drink, and stretching. Remember your warm-up while training? Now you'll feel the full benefit of a few relaxing stretches. On the first stop, adjust your boots (maybe loosening the laces) and straighten socks. Loosen a tight bra or belt. You might need to make an adjustment in your pack if, for instance, it's heavier on one side than on the other.

When starting out on a hike from a rest stop or climbing a steep section of trail, I have found it helpful to hyperventilate—i.e., force breathing in and out for a minute or two at a faster than normal rate. Maybe it's because I live at sea level most of the time or maybe it's because of my age, but hyperventilating helps me get going—like choking a car when starting up on a cold morning. It puts extra oxygen into my lungs just ahead of the body's message and thus keeps me from panting. I'm sure I conserve energy this way.

Even though you are in good shape and you've done the advance training, your first steep hill climb with a pack will come as quite a revelation. No doubt some of these suggestions will come flooding back. Just remember to slow down, hyperventilate, and then, breathing rhythmically, walk with short steps.

When walking uphill, avoid contracting your calf muscles and force-lifting your heel too far up and off the ground. It expends too much energy; just let your foot roll forward and use your thighs to lift your weight.

It may surprise you to learn that walking downhill is not going to be the great relief you expected. Though less demanding on your motor and horsepower, it is not the dream you hoped for. On every step, you expend a great deal of effort holding yourself back. This effort takes a lot of muscle energy— from a different set of muscles, however, than those used for uphill climbs. Your heel strikes the ground first, and then there is a large distance for the toe to travel before it hits terra firma. The shin muscles have to take up the slack, and eventually they get tired and stiff, especially if you have been wearing high heels most of your life. Then sometimes there is loose rock or tufted grass to twist ankles and play hell with the balance of a pack. Your motor and wind (heart and lungs) machine won't be laboring, but your "suspension and shocks" (knee and ankle joints) will. A considerate leader will plan frequent stops on the way down, too. Having done the fourteen-day training course I suggested earlier in Chapter 4, you'll know the stretches to do in order to relieve and revitalize any sore muscles.

If you are a city person and your youthful romps have been limited to playgrounds and seashore camps, I have some useful tips that should help you maneuver over the variety of wilderness and mountain terrains you'll encounter on your way to the top. If you are country bred, reading this advice will refresh your memory.

On normal mountain expeditions, you will seldom need to cross wide rivers. (If you make your beginner's trip with NOLS or Outward Bound, they will teach you how a group crosses wide, deep rivers safely with the use of ropes.) But you probably will encounter shallow streams in your path that you must cross by wading with your pack. A smart woman on her first hike will hold back and let others pick their way first, so she can find the safest, shallowest route. There may be sand to sink into or unseen deep potholes. Now is the time to pick up a stout stick or branch 5 or 6 feet long so you have the extra support of a three-legged tripod. Then undo your pack's waistbelt. If you fall, you want to be free to slip out of the shoulder straps. The weight of the pack will help you keep your balance in a fast-rushing stream. Your hiking/climbing boots should be worn when you are wading with packs—you need the protection and support. And mountain streams are icy, so leave your socks on and change into a dry pair on the other side. The water, as you've learned, will not hurt your boots if you avoid drying them in the sun or by the fire. Just pour the water out, wipe them dry, and put on fresh socks. In fact, you may find that wading cools hot feet and refits tight boots better than before. It certainly cannot unfit them if you continue to wear them until they are dry. If you have only one pair of socks, your best solution is to remove your socks, put your boots on bare feet, lace them as tightly as possible, cross the stream, wipe your boots dry, and then put your dry socks back on. Caution—lace unsocked boots tightly. You need the support, and you cannot afford to step out of a stuck boot and lose it to the current.

Most rocks around streams or rivers will be worn

smooth, so you can't expect the great traction you've been getting with Vibram soles on dry rock with a textured surface. When stepping from wet rock to wet rock, place each foot very carefully before shifting your weight. It may be more exciting to leap from boulder to boulder and reach the other bank dry and ready to go, but if you slip and have to struggle to recover your balance, you use a lot of energy you might need later in the day—better to wade on the bottom and have wet feet for a few minutes.

To minimize the energy loss in case you do lose your balance, lean forward slightly. If you slip, it will probably be backwards; you'll be thrown into an upright position and can recover. If you are straight up to begin with, your feet will go forward and you will be thrown onto your back. When going uphill, it's best to walk perpendicular to a gravitational horizontal line—i.e., head and shoulders straight up toward the sky. You are then balanced to recover against a step that would throw you forward.

You may encounter a spot at the base of a mountain where nature, eons before, has thrown a field of boulders down onto your path. It might be safe enough and faster on these dry rocks to step from boulder to boulder. Always try to step on the high point of boulders, as you are less likely to unbalance them this way. If you move from top to top, you can see your next moves better. Also, by staying on top you are usually moving on the heaviest rocks, which are least likely to move under your weight. Small boulders or rocks on a hillside are most apt to come unbalanced with your weight.

Basically, in all situations, think conservatively—think of you. Earlier, I suggested that you go with

co-ed groups for two reasons: to encounter your own reactions to unfamiliar men, boys and women, and to learn to function for your own benefit, not just out of the social habits that are familiar and without serious consequence in domestic life. Since you have no measure of your outdoor skills or endurance, it is better to adapt a selfish, cautious approach in the beginning. You must temporarily overcome your normal social instincts to please or to "keep up" in order to limit the danger of injury or fatigue.

8 | THE CAMP AND TENT SITE

Force issues out of order.

—Taine

Your expedition leader will decide when to stop for the night. After he or she picks the tent site and performs the first *and last* demonstration of how to set up a tent, you and your tentmate will be on your own to select a spot. For those setting up a tent for the first time, the experience can be like a Chinese puzzle. If you haven't done it before, nothing else in your experience will clue you in. So no matter how tired or bored you are that first evening, concentrate on your leader's every word and move to save yourself fatiguing frustration later. Take all the help and advice you can get the first few days out. After all, you're there to learn, not to compete. And you must save energy. Just resolve that you'll go the last half of the trip without taking advantage of unnecessary "crutches"—even ones that are six feet tall with P. Newman "blues."

That first day out you'll no doubt stop early to allow plenty of daylight for setting up tents, cooking, and generally making the wilderness adaptation that you were not able to fully experience on the trail. Nothing is more annoying to the inexperienced camper than

117

trying to set up and cook after dark. Irritability and accidents will result. Many women especially appreciate getting far off the trail so that they are not disturbed by strange hikers while doing camp chores.

It is human nature to want to pick a marvelous, inspiring view, but there are a few principles that should take precedence: safety, conservation, comfort. In that order!

You need shelter from the elements, but "tenting" close beneath a steep bank or cliff could leave you in jeopardy of falling rocks. Check trees around you to be sure you're not in the path of dead limbs or trunks that might blow over during the night. Aboveground roots or branches that might stab the eye in the dark are also to be avoided. Picture-window perches at the edge of sheer drop-offs afford impressive views, but unless you are rock climbing and have no choice, what's the point? A nighttime emergency could result with one false step.

Camp away from lakeshores; the ecological destruction you wreak by camping near the water is too great. Besides, you'll avoid more insects. Meadows, giant forests, and small streams are just as pleasant. Don't tent in a field of flowers unless you are sure they're the kind that will recover next year. Incidentally, if you bring any disposable items that are not biodegradable, be prepared to carry them out in small sacks. Nothing disturbs the beauty of the wilderness more quickly than the sight of people litter.

A level spot on a hillside is hard to find, but it's worth any effort to assure a good night's sleep—especially the first night. If you've been conscientious about training, outfitting correct boots, and conserving energy by rhythmic breathing, small steps, and careful water crossings, don't blow it now. If your tent and bed slope sideways, you're going to engage in a semiconscious wrestle with downhill gravity, and you'll be grouchy and tired the next day. If your head is lower than your feet, you won't be able to fall asleep. If you can't avoid a slope, at least put your head uphill. But inhabitants of a two-person tent generally sleep foot-to-head for best harmony, which means that one of them has to build a pillow out of clothing or other gear for the upper part of the body; and this makes it uncomfortable to roll on one's side. It may be that you won't know a spot is not level until it's too late. Lie down before you set up your tent just to test the area. This will help you locate hidden roots, stumps and branches. It's worth any effort to make it level. Borrow the camp shovel, if necessary, and pile up pine needles and leaves.

To ensure a good, refreshing full night's rest, you have to consider the possibility of a strong wind and rain coming up after dark and causing tent noise or leaking to wake you. A row of bushes or trees, the leeward side of a rock pile, or a giant boulder will make a good screen. The banks of a dry gully may seem like an ideal windscreen, but a quick storm with heavy rains could cause flash flooding during the night and make your tent into a Noah's Ark before daylight.

The tent you'll use will probably be either a two-person nylon mountain tent or what is commonly referred to as a rain fly, also made of nylon. Strung between trees, it is only high enough to crawl under. A piece of waterproof plastic is laid out next to the ground, then a padding of foam sheeting, and the sleeping bag on top. Down-filled jackets and other pieces of clothing are also useful as padding beneath your sleeping bag.

Your leader will probably pick an open spot for the cooking fire and suggest that you hikers pitch your tents in the forest, both for protection and to take advantage of ground padding from tree leaves and debris. Have your tent at least 25 feet from fire to avoid smoke and falling sparks—the distance should be even greater if you are downwind. The tent entrance should be downwind, too.

If you grew up in a family of Boy Scouts or were an active Girl Scout yourself, you may have had a chance to learn some knots that will serve you well now. If not, consult a Boy Scout manual for a few simple knots that will hold but can be undone as simply as a shoelace knot. The Boy Scout handbook of 1965 or one of more recent vintage is the second most useful reading matter available to a woman starting her first hiking and climbing experience. (You already own the number-one book!) They can often be picked up at secondhand sales for twenty-five cents. The Girl Scout handbooks I've seen do not have as much outdoor information as the Boy Scout handbooks. Maybe recent ones are more complete, but they will not be a bargain. Pitching a tent or fly requires tying support strings to logs, pegs and branches, but not so tight that cold, wet fingers in a high wind cannot undo them. A simple bow knot, like a shoelace knot tied double, will work. Illustrated are the sheet bend and two half hitches. You'll learn special knots later when you get into rock climbing and rappelling.

Remember that branches or sticks that blow in the wind can make a hole in your tent wall. At best, you can only tape a tear or worn spot temporarily. If a tear starts at an end, however, it can be tied off before it enlarges.

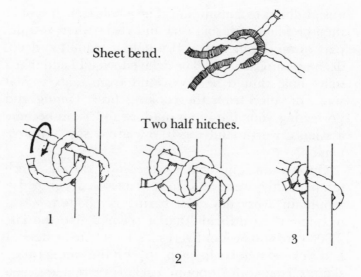

Sheet bend.

Two half hitches.

1

2

3

While you've been setting up a tent, your leader has most likely been digging a toilet trench for the campers. He or she will probably assign that duty to a different person each evening. Since it will be your chore to dig or fill one day, you might want to know the reason. Human feces are buried in order to prevent pollution from bacteria. An outdoor toilet is the first order of business once a decision about a campsite has been made. Conversely, it is the last order attended to before leaving the next day. The spot picked should be on high ground some distance from any streams or lakes so that rainwater will be filtered before it seeps to lower levels. Toilet holes must never be in low swampy spots or near water. The hole should be dug as a trench 10 to 15 inches deep. The shovel should then be left nearby so that each user can throw a thin covering of soil over the waste and the paper in order to keep odor and unsightliness to a minimum. The whole trench should then be filled with soil, turf and rocks when you depart camp the next day. If a hole is made too deep, decomposing action will be delayed. Need I add that a toilet hole should be downwind from tents and at some distance from the cooking fire? Timing and perfecting your use of an outdoor toilet can become a science worth studying if you are a shy, sensitive person.

Once, on a long winter expedition during which temperatures were at zero and below, I climbed a mountain every day. Just baring my bottom was a movement so difficult that it seemed like the last 2,000 yards on Mount Everest. Yet it had to be done. I had to keep regular to keep up with the young turks, skiing all day with 70-pound packs (I carried less even with cameras). I spent hours figuring out how to outwit my body plumbing so that action could happen in the last sunlight in case I missed the morning. Nibbling pinches of raw bran and snow from noon on, followed by hot tea at the first evening fire, usually allowed me to beat the setting sun. The others settled for the cold and dark before crawling inside tents. The expedition wasn't spectacular, but I had a personal "high" just from being regular. I felt like the rookie of the year batting 500.

In trying to decide whether to write about this subject or ignore it, I remembered several women on a summer hike—one so sensitive that she waited until everyone had gone to bed; then with a small flashlight, she made her way to the toilet hole. After the whole camp had turned in one very dark night, there was a blood-curdling scream. Everyone leaped up to discover that "Betty Braille" had touched "Florence

Flashlight" at the toilet hole. They were shocked and embarrassed but later became good friends. Together they invented a simple signal to indicate whether the "ditch" was in use day or night: A bandanna was attached to a 6-foot limb and placed at the intersection of the camp and the path to the toilet hole. If the ditch was in use, the branch was standing with the bandanna at the top; if not in use, it would just lie across the path, to remind others to hoist it for privacy.

It would be bad manners and poor conservation practice for hikers to dig private holes all over the landscape. The "public facility" in the woods just takes a little getting used to. A woman should not hesitate to criticize a leader who puts the toilet too close to the cooking area or the tents. If you're a night person, try to pitch your tent on the same side as the facility so you won't telegraph your destination by tripping over tent pegs on the way.

Disposing of tampons is not a problem. Tampax, for example, is biodegradable because it is mostly paper, and could be buried. Most women carry sanitary napkins only when there is heavy bleeding, and these could be burned or carried out in a plastic bag.

9 | FIRES AND COOKING DINNER

Great effects with little means.

—Beethoven

If you are starting your first camping experience, a few principles of "firewomanship" will help you adapt to the difference between cooking with gas or electricity in your kitchen and preparing food over an open wood fire. For what it's worth in the trivia department, I've noticed that in the beginning, men do a better job on open wood fires; women are better cooks with the small portable stoves. But no matter who is cooking or how bad it is, you're going to eat it; if it is especially good, for field cooking, be sure to compliment the chef. Nothing adds so much zest to a day in the wild outdoors as a super dish at dinner; and flavor is important, since those dinners are all going to be served without cocktails or wine.

If you're with an experienced group, they will know whether fires are permitted in the area you're hiking in and whether you need a fire permit. But you would do well to check this out with the ranger or sheriff who marked your maps before you left town. Conservation and fire prevention suggest that we always assume conditions for forest fires to be at their best. Take precautions each time.

125

Clay soil, real earth and rock don't burn, except in some low bottomlands. Generally, if you scrape away enough top litter from the ground, you'll get down to nonburnable soil. Then dig a fire pit about 15×24×8 inches deep on level ground. One end should be deeper for dumping dishwater and excess food. Scrape forest litter away from the pit edges. Pick up large litter in a wide ring around the pit—6 to 8 feet. Debris and extra firewood should be stacked several feet from the fire pit. Save the topsoil and turf to be replaced later. Keep the food preparation area 5 to 6 feet from the fire. A handy log or a big rock will save you some stooping, but avoid moving rocks to ring a fire. Besides leaving the area looking burned and scarred for life, moving rocks from some ancient setting upsets a chain of cell life unnecessarily. Line the floor of the fire pit with an inch or two of small litter, sticks and pine needles to insulate against the damp earth. This will help sustain small, early flames when you are starting a fire with twigs. It's best to use wood matches to light a small pile of pine needles, dead leaves, grass, bark and matchstick-size litter that is placed on top of the fire-pit floor for insulation padding. Use cigarette-size sticks only after starting the fire with matchstick- and toothpick-size sticks. Keep a little pile nearby to feed one at a time as the flames increase.

When you have put on quite a few of cigarette size and each is flaming, you can start adding larger pieces gradually. Study the effect of position and note how quickly and how well each type of wood burns. No one can teach you—you will learn by diligence and attention. Firemaking can become an art for the woman who will concentrate patiently and learn from experience.

When you have accumulated a supply of coals, separate them from the flame area at one end of the pit. Thus you will have two kinds of heat to cook with, plus a steady supply of new coals. Coals are usually best for both cooking and cleaning. The fire must be constantly attended. It's a good idea to pour some water on the ground around the fire pit to retard eco-destruction.

This type of fire is made for cooking, not for heat. Use clothing for warmth, except in emergencies, when you should choose a large rock or a hillside to act as a heat reflector, and position yourself so that the cold camper is between the fire and the reflector. Above timberline, you'll need a mountain stove; or take food that doesn't need cooking if your stay is going to be brief.

After you have started the fire and before you begin the food preparation, put some kindling into a plastic bag or inside your tent for the breakfast fire. It takes a long time—maybe an hour—to get a cooking fire ready, but the other campers will not have been idle and you will need the time to arrange the cooking area and to prepare the food for cooking. Even before you decide on the menu, start a large pot of water to heat on the first coals. If you're having dehydrated vegetables, they should have already been put into a pot with a little water and salt to presoak for an hour.

Teaching women to cook—in the field or anywhere else—is not a subject I feel qualified for, so you'll get no master chef lessons on these pages. I want only to give you some hints about handling the mechanics with the fewest accidents, and about cleaning up with unfamiliar materials, plus some theory about food for expeditions.

Handle hot cook pots with pot grippers while wearing cotton gloves. When you want to season or add something to a dish, first remove the dish from the fire. Those who are not cooking should stand back, so that you never have to pass the hot pot over someone. To balance a pot or a can on coals, sometimes you may have to stick in a green limb or small stones. Besides gloves and pot grippers, you'll need one large frying pan with a lid (Teflon is recommended); two tin cans, number 10 size, or a nesting set; one collapsible 2½-gallon water jug and two plastic quart bottles, all to be filled from a nearby water supply when you start cooking. You'll also want your own personal spoon, cup and bowl for eating.

You can bake in a frying pan by setting the pan on a bed of coals and putting hot coals on the lid. The bed of coals should feel hot, but not burning hot, when you hold your hand about six inches above it. If you can keep it there a few seconds without discomfort, it is the right temperature for baking. The coals on the lid should be kept even hotter.

Another method is to put the smaller of two nesting cans with a lid on top of four or five small rocks in the bottom of the larger can with a lid. It helps to build a small fire of twigs on the lid of the large can. With water between the cans, this will work as a double boiler.

Cook in clean pots. Old food stuck on pans or pots will burn and will spoil the flavor of the food you're preparing. A bland taste usually means a lack of salt. Start with sufficient water and check to keep it supplied. Cook on low fire heat. Stir thickened foods often. Poor timing of a combination of ingredients usually results in overcooking some of them. If mixing, add freeze-dried foods first; cook them 10 to 12 minutes at a boil; then you're ready for rice or pasta. You can tell if it's done only by the taste. Milk and cheese should be added last, just before dish is done, because they tend to burn if put in too soon.

Food must be clearly identifiable in its packages — color coded or labeled or stored in clear plastic bags. Freezer-size bags are best. Don't fill them to the top; leave room to tie them in a loose knot. Then all plastic bags can be carried in what is commonly called a "stuff sack," usually made of nylon with a long zipper pocket. All the food can be stored in one bag, and several people can use it or alternate carrying it without confusion.

Even though a woman's body fuels more efficiently than a man's, you will need more carbohydrates on an expedition than you are used to. The strenuous activity of hiking requires greater than normal amounts of energy. Although you've been taught to fear and hate them as a woman's enemy, fats and carbohydrates are the most efficient foods to supply extra energy. Sugar and starches are quick-energy foods that give your body an added boost soon after intake, but the energy from fats, although slower acting, is longer lasting. Eaten at dinnertime, before sleep, fats help keep you warm through the night. In your city life, you may have avoided eating for long periods or learned to ignore hunger pangs to keep slim. Now, on an expedition, you should eat whenever you feel the need; and don't cut back on quantity, especially in cold weather.

Of course you need a variety of proteins, too. These, eaten with fats and some carbohydrates, provide the best energy source. Protein foods take some careful planning, because they are not so easy to carry. Meat has to be dried, eggs and milk powdered.

Cheese is ideal to carry; so are nuts (peanuts, hazel-nuts, Brazil nuts and walnuts are cheaper by bulk than are cashews and almonds). And if you're near a high mountain lake, fresh trout will provide not only protein but a special taste. Of course you'd need to be a fly fisherwoman—and that's another book—or to have one in the party. With all the powdered proteins available, including milk, eggs, cheese and dried meat or substitutes, you don't need to worry about fresh fish. You'll need two main meals a day, consisting of the four food groups: (1) proteins, such as meat, fish, powdered eggs and nuts; (2) cereals and grains; (3) milk and cheese (for calcium); (4) fruits and vegetables (apples and oranges travel well); plus margarine, and candy or honey.

Although most modern women avoid too much salt because they know it causes the body to retain water and leads to kidney problems later in life, a different outlook is advisable on hiking and climbing expeditions, where the body needs both salt and water in balance. Strenuous exercise, high body temperatures and high altitude deplete one's salt supply. Susceptibility to frostbite and even hypoglycemia can result from dehydration. Altitude and mountain sickness can best be avoided by a proper salt and water balance. Salt pills from the drugstore scare me because I cannot estimate the dosage or quantity. Besides, they have a heavy taste. Rock salt crystals always seem easier to regulate, and I can spread out my intake. Start with no more than two to five crystals a day. I have found that for me it works to add one more crystal for every 1,000 feet above 5,000. If you sweat a lot, on some days you could easily double your normal intake. Force yourself to drink water frequently. As you gain altitude, the air is drier, especially—and surprisingly—in the winter. You will need a quarter to a third more water than in summer (two to three quarts a day). Try to take care of your salt needs at mealtimes and your water needs on the trail.

Now, assume you've tasted your presalted, dehydrated vegetables that have been cooking and you're ready to add some chunks from a meat bar, plus a couple of squares of beef bouillon, some pepper and oregano. Stir well; then add more off-center coals to the fire, and make room for another pot to cook macaroni and cheese. You may want to finish off dinner with an apple, or a dehydrated fruit such as peaches. After you have finished cooking, the coals can be scattered in the fire pit and left to burn out. When the pots and dishes have been cleaned, pour some more water on the ground around the pit to keep the heat down, to eliminate damage to the earth, and to prevent the fire from spreading. The end of the fire pit that is lower and deeper is for disposing of dishwater and nonburnable garbage.

Those of you who pride yourselves on your housekeeping and sanitary dishwashing methods will no doubt be surprised that I don't use soap or detergents to clean pots or bowls while on an expedition. Sanitation is important to prevent diarrhea, especially if one is hoping to climb a difficult peak. One's own germs may affect others, but they rarely hurt their carrier. Cooking gear should be cleaned before and after using by sterilizing with boiling water for ten to fifteen minutes. Soap itself, if not properly rinsed off cooking gear, can cause diarrhea as well as spoiling the flavor of the food. Use natural ground litter— pine needles, grass or gravel—in place of scouring pads. Avoid washing dishes directly in a stream or lake. Don't worry about a perfect cleaning after eating; there will always be traces of food or grease, and germs will develop during the heat of the day in transit. Cheese and macaroni will stick to pots, resisting your best efforts. Put cold water into those pots and let them stand overnight; the resulting gluck will come off more easily. A frying pan can be boiled out with water. Scraping with a stick will clean the seams in a billy can. Don't let others use your eating utensils or your spoon. (A metal spoon can be burned over a flame for sterilization.) The personal hygiene of the cook is very important.

Biodegradable soap should be used for washing the hands after using the toilet and before handling food. Fingernails should be kept clean. It is very hard to keep long fingernails on a wilderness trip; I don't recommend trying. Cut and trim them before packing, and maybe paint them with a hardener for added protection and strength. My wife buffs hers thoroughly and uses two coats of ceramic glaze by Fabergé. She doesn't carry it with her, though.

10 | THE NIGHT —
SLEEPING BAG

Fatigue is the best pillow.

—Benjamin Franklin

You have washed your dishes, cleaned the cook pots, refilled the water bottles, stored some dry wood for the morning fire, put the food into your pack, and tied the flap against rain or the rare animal thief— squirrel, chipmunk—and now you are ready to crawl into your tent and sleeping bag for your first night in the wild. You will now find it's equally important to get a very good night's sleep to store up enough energy for another day. Probably you will travel a greater distance, over steeper and rougher terrain, and at higher and colder levels than you did today. A good, comfortable night is vital!

What are your chances?

Pretty good if you're not overtired, constipated, dehydrated, uncomfortably dirty, cold, hyper-nervous, overstimulated by the day's activities, or suffering from claustrophobia; or if you're not a princess who can feel a pea under her mattress.

Some random hints follow.

Since there will probably be two of you in a two-person tent, it would be advantageous to discuss the details of sharing; that is, who gets which side or who

133

sleeps with her head at the entrance. (As I've said earlier, it seems to work out best to sleep head-to-toe so you are not breathing each other's exhaust. Foot movements in the night are not so disturbing to a tentmate as shifting shoulders and hips.) A woman will appreciate a few moments of privacy even in a space where one cannot stand up, hang a mirror, sit on a stool, switch on a light, or plug in a hair dryer. So, work out who gets what period for private tent time.

You will leave your backpack outside, propped against a tree, with the flap tied to protect the contents against sudden wind and rain. Take inside the tent clothes you'll want for the next day and anything you might want during the night. Before you crawl in, brush your clothes free of leaves, sand and twigs. Leave your camp shoes just inside the tent door, with flashlight, eyeglasses and pocketknife tucked inside them. Some people prefer to keep a flashlight inside their sleeping bag. If you want a flashlight with you, be sure you can lock the switch in the OFF position to avoid accidentally turning it on and burning out the batteries. A simple homemade solution is a piece of tape which you can restick over the switch in the OFF position each time you use it. Extra clothing can be used as a pillow underneath the head of the bag. Even food items make a good headrest (the best pillow I ever had was a food sack with rice, grain and peanuts on top). After you've stepped out of your clothes— except maybe underpants and T-shirt for summer sleeping—and padded the bottom of the bag, you may want to attend to a few personal tasks such as brushing your hair, cleaning your face with a little alcohol-soaked cotton before patting on cream or oil (be sure to wipe off the excess before putting your face down on the sleeping bag, or use a small face towel to protect the nylon). The Boy Scout or Swiss army knife has handy blades to clean your nails if you cannot locate that nail file even with your diary and compass. Massage and clean your feet with alcohol. Check your toenails and any sore spots for blisters, and treat any problems. Maybe you'll need to oil the insides of your boots to soften up spots that are rubbing. You'll only discover blisters ahead of time if you examine your two feet closely. Lots of people use contact lenses these days. If you do, be sure you bring an extra set. Carry them in a special container around your neck. Have the extra container around your neck at night to hold the pair you're wearing. When you remove them, set them in the center of your smoothed-out sleeping bag, with a flashlight on your lap so you don't have to crawl around if you should drop a lens. Campfire smoke irritates the eyes, and even women without contacts enjoy using a refreshing eyewash before sleeping. (Liquid Tear is a brand I recommend; my wife uses Eye D.) If you have not camped near a stream or lake in which you can bathe, at least change into fresh undies and shirt the first night; you'll feel fresher. Check your watch—you should be ready for your sleeping bag. It's probably only 9 P.M. and just getting dark. Go outside for one last kidney break, but avoid people and stimulating discussions with the group who hang around the fire pit.

Sleeping Bag

Yours will probably be the "mummy bag" type, so named because when you are in it you resemble the ancient Egyptian mummies buried in the pyramids. The main attraction is that, by tying a drawstring at the neck position, you can seal in your entire body including your head, with only the nose and mouth exposed. A woman inside will stay quite warm simply by containing her own body heat. I have slept in snow caves in January on top of the Tetons when it was forty below and never felt cold. I was fully dressed inside the bag, with several sweaters, plus long Johns and three pairs of socks, and with my bag on top of an Ensolite pad on top of a ground sheet on top of pure snow. I used a zippered nylon mummy bag filled with Dacron and made by the Paul Petzoldt Wilderness Equipment Company. Dacron for bags and outer clothing is preferable to down because of one valuable safety feature: Like wool, even when it is wet it provides insulation and allows the body to breathe. There are many stories of campers caught in a sudden rain that turned to freezing snow in the mountains who could not use wet down-filled sleeping bags. Keeping sleeping bags dry and aired, fluffed and free of tears could mean survival. It's wise to remember that if you're ever suddenly chilled, as from falling into a river or stream, you should get inside your bag with or without wet clothes and stay until you regain your normal body temperature.

When you crawl inside your bag to sleep at night, it will feel fresh and pleasant if it is free of sand, leaves and insects because you've taken the trouble to shake it out and hang it on the tent or trees for an hour or two to air. You can control the temperature inside by the amount of space you leave around your face and shoulders and the amount of clothing you have on. Start with only a T-shirt in summer, but have a sweater handy. The night usually gets colder as it wears on. If you are one of the fastidious types I mentioned earlier, spend a few minutes staring into the flames of the fire or looking at the constellations above before retiring. Consciously turn your mind down; think only of pleasant scenes from the past; do not think about the next day or worry that you may have lost some item or tool. Be confident that in fresh daylight everything will show up. Relax.

There is a certain feeling of confinement in a sleeping bag that disturbs some people. In fact, I admit to certain claustrophobic feelings myself on the first nights. You cannot spread out, as you can on a bed; you cannot sleep on your side very well. So, if you move from the supine position, you encounter frustration. It is difficult to read by flashlight, but if it's your habit and you're having trouble getting to sleep, try it. A good night's sleep is well worth a set of batteries on any mountain expedition. If it's cold or you're on a winter climb, be sure to take some nibbling food to bed. I would wake up on cold nights at two in the morning and need some fuel in my furnace. M&M's mixed with peanuts and dried apricots were my favorite. I cannot ever remember having any problem with mosquitoes at night. I suspect that as you go to higher altitudes, the cold nighttime temperature puts them in deep freeze until the sunny daylight hours.

If you can manage to get through the night without a kidney call, your night will be more restful. If you do have to leave your tent, be sure to put on at least your camp footwear, and put some distance between you and the other tents. Urination is a minor inconvenience, but it can be odorific.

Apropos smells, a woman should leave antiperspirants, perfumes and colognes at home. They add unnecessary weight, and the scents serve only to attract insects in the daytime. I've even heard it rumored that bears are attracted to strange scents.

If you do leave your tent at night for some reason, no need to hurry back inside. Take a breather; sit on a rock and watch the moonlight on the water, or study the stars and feel the quiet. Part of the reason you got yourself into this world was to experience the "call of the wild." Check your watch; it might be only a short while to sunrise. If you've slept well, you might want to catch that sight. If you're like most city people, you saw your first and last sunrise on the night of your high school prom. Even if it was only a few weeks ago, the setting of skyscrapers and rooftops does not compare with pines and snow-covered peaks. Besides, at first light the fish and game begin to stir. This is your best chance to see moose, elk, deer, bobcats, lynx, beavers, owls, and much more.

In anticipation of the experience, if you haven't done so already, make the acquaintance of Annie Dillard. Read her book *Pilgrim at Tinker Creek*. She will teach you how to observe the details of nature as though you had a "binoculars-microscope sandwich" in your head.

11 | BREAKFAST AND BREAKING CAMP

And if you've brought your electric toothbrush, just plug it into a wild currant bush.

—Ruth Dyar Mendenhall

You shift your derrière. You feel the hard knob of a root beneath you and the padding you stuffed under your sleeping bag. Then your improvised pillow needs adjustment, and you open one eye to discover, not the dark of night, but a world bathed in cerulean blue. The sunlight outside the tent casts a nylon blue over your tentmate and clothes, creating the soft movie mood of a sheik's tent—Lawrence of Arabia or Valentino?

The romance is short-lived. Your ears pick up foot sounds, and your bladder feels full to bursting. You loosen the drawstring and sit up in your mummy bag to put on a wool shirt. That done, you remember your pants under your feet. Now, on top of the sleeping bag, you must squirm into the pants without standing. Your tentmate begins to stir, but you've slid to your tent door and put on socks and boots (after removing the flashlight and the pocketknife). Without lacing or tying the boots, you've crawled out and stumbled into the bushes. Disgruntled, disheveled, disoriented, you utter a huge sigh of relief and stand up to a yawn and

140

a stretch that tell you where every muscle is. Your feet feel stiff and awkward; your calves are lumps, your thighs and buttocks cramped. Your back, from spine to neck, groans. Even your neck and shoulders hurt, but you're alive—and feeling smugly proud at the moment, if the truth were told. "You Are Woman," as Helen Reddy sings. You look around, smiling like some primitive queen surveying her tribe.

Another "Eve" is starting a fire crouched on her knees and blowing the flames under a little stick teepee Indian style. At that instant she lets out a war whoop, shouting, "One match! Look, Mom, no hands—just one match!" The rest of the expedition are awake and moving. Some are scrubbing their teeth, others pouring water into coffee cups. One is dragging out her sleeping bag to air in the sun before stuffing it into its sack for travel. Your leader already has her tent down and is rolling it with practiced economy into a neat package. Feeling like family, strangers of yesterday now banter and smile, at ease. The teen-marines are running back from a freezing plunge into the lake, snapping towels at one another's shriveled, unprotected parts: a vanishing locker-room ritual not yet outgrown.

This morning, breakfast is oatmeal, made very simply: 4 cups of water and ½ teaspoon of salt brought to a boil; 2 cups of cereal sprinkled in slowly, cooked about 2 minutes. You add brown sugar and your palate is pleased. Soon you smell the powdered scrambled eggs that have been mixed with powdered milk and water in a frying pan, along with 2 table-spoons of melted butter. Add 2 cups of coffee each, with cookies, cake and bread that have lasted since yesterday.

The last of the coals are stirred around in the fire

pit to give them a chance to burn out. Everyone has eaten; everyone is satisfied. Packing and garbage clean-up are done while the coals are still smoldering. Paper in the toilet is burned before the waste is covered with soil, litter, rocks and finally turf. Then the coals in the fire pit are doused with lots of water, and extra water is poured on to cool and remoisten the surrounding ground. Some ash and coals may be left in the pit, but most should be burned in a separate place or, if completely dead, spread over the grass and fields. The original soil must be replaced to bring it up to ground level. Extra water should be poured on to recharge the disturbed vegetation. Debris should be spread over the widened fire-pit area again in a manner that will disguise its recent use to the casual observer. Now your duty is complete and you can move on, already feeling suppleness replacing the stiffness of the night, created by warmth of a windbreaker contouring the heat of your body, now in action again.

12 | NAVIGATION

Those who wish to succeed must first ask the right preliminary questions.

—Aristotle

You are a couple of days away from so-called civilization. But if you have not been following your progress on a topographical map of the area, you really don't know exactly where your feet are planted at this very moment. With a map, in clear daylight, and with some practice, you can locate yourself anywhere.

If you are making your expedition with a professionally led group, learning map reading is not necessary as an advance preparation. The people and schools listed in this book will teach that skill in the field as part of their program. However, the time will come when you will want to make an expedition into an unfamiliar area, perhaps with a group of friends also with limited experience. Going into strange country on your own, after you've had your first expedition, can be one of this life's great adventures. You'll go back in time to pioneer ancestors and feel some of the excitement of those early explorers. You'll know what Balboa felt when he first sighted the Pacific Ocean.

143

After you've decided on a destination, you'll need your topographical map. Simply write to the U.S. Geological Survey at one of the following offices:

1028 GSA Bldg.
18th & F Sts., NW
Washington, D.C.   20242

8102 Federal Office Bldg.
125 South State
Salt Lake City, Utah   84111

Denver Federal Center, Bldg. 41
Denver, Colorado   80225

345 Middlefield Rd.
Menlo Park, California   94025

Room W-2235
Federal Bldg.
2800 Cottage Way
'Sacramento, California   95825

Room 504
Custom House
555 Battery St.
San Francisco, California   94111

Ask for an index map of the state in question. It will identify regions covered by individual maps and facilitate ordering the correct maps. Also ask for a guide to topographical map symbols, which will help others in your party learn to read them, too.

Topographical maps are not complicated, and you should not be scared off or disturbed by the maze of lines in front of you. They may seem confusing until you've waded through the hours of study and practice necessary to pick up the highlights. But then you can use shortcut techniques.

Topographical maps are very accurate. Based on aerial photographs, they put you in the position of looking straight down at the ground you are walking over—from a "plane's-eye" view at 30,000 feet.

The scale of map most commonly used by hikers is 1:24,000. A distance of one inch on this kind of map means a distance of 2,000 feet in the field; $1/4$ inch equals 500 feet; that is, about 2 $5/8$ inches on the map equals one mile on the ground. To figure distance, simply consult the mileage scale at the bottom of the map. Then mark that length on the side of your pencil, or break a twig or a pine needle to size. You can measure one mile at a time over the route you want to travel.

Now you need only to learn to measure vertical elevation by the contours. Marked in wavy brown lines that connect points on the ground surface that have the same elevation, they are spaced by a contour interval. The number of vertical feet between contour lines or intervals is noted at the bottom of the map.

Just these two distances can tell you how long it will take you to reach a certain destination if you have the experience to judge your group's walking speed over the terrain the map now reveals. Climbing 250 feet in elevation will take as much energy as walking one flat mile—5,280 feet. Obviously, contour lines very close together on the map indicate very steep going. For example, if the horizontal distance is 50 feet and the vertical distance close to 50 feet also, you may need to use rock-climbing techniques, with ropes, belays, etc. It might be wise to walk around. Notice that contour lines crossing streams always form a V that points upstream. Contour lines form Vs on the sides of hills and mountains. The point of the V is the valley or coltier, and the sides are ridges.

When you have learned to recognize symbol shorthand and the natural landmarks on a topographical map, you'll be able to orient the map to your actual position without a compass. Just find peaks and lakes you can identify, and match them to the configuration on the map by turning the map. The top will be at true north.

When you are sure you have the correct map for the trip you've planned and have studied the routes in general, you may want to iron a cloth backing—such as the kind for patching clothes—onto the map and then spray the map with waterproof plastic. It will then survive weather and abuse.

Next, you should get a compass. A compass is invaluable in snowstorms or fog, or in forests where no mountains or landmarks are visible. Remember, however, that the needle points to magnetic north, not true north. You must find the compass direction at the bottom of the topographical map, as it varies in different regions. Take note of the correction degrees from magnetic north to true north as shown on the map. A compass reading is distorted by the proximity of metal objects, so take your reading at least 20 feet from your car and 10 feet from axes or knives.

If you are using a contour map daily on your expedition, studying terrain and landmarks as you go, a compass is almost superfluous except when you are consulting your map. I find that when I see the compass placed directly on the route, its accuracy helps me to orient myself to the map. The best compasses for topographical map use are made by the Silva

Company. They also are the official Boy Scout compasses and are available at most sporting goods stores; or you can write Silva, Inc., Highway 39, North La Porte, Indiana 46350. Don't spend more than $10 for a compass.

You can also find true north without a compass. Lay your watch on a stone or on the ground and position a wooden match upright against the edge of the watch. Twist the watch so that its shadow falls precisely along the hour hand, with the hour hand pointing directly at the sun. Now divide in half the angle between the hour hand and the number 12 on the dial. Between 6 A.M. and 6 P.M. Standard Time, a line from the center of the watch through the halfway mark between the hour hand and the 12 will point to true south. Scratch a line on the ground straight out from the center of your watch, and you have your north-south line. If your watch is on Daylight Saving Time, use the same method but divide the angle between the hour hand and the number 1 to find south.

At nighttime, use the North Star to find true north. Just draw an imaginary line from the star to the ground, and mark the ground with a branch for later use in daylight. First, find the Big Dipper: Four stars that form a bowl; add three to make the handle. Use the two stars of the bowl farthest from the handle— called the "Pointers"—to guide you to the North Star—called Polaris—which is at the end of the handle of the Little Dipper beneath it. You'll recognize the North Star; it is brighter and larger than the others.

If you're like my daughters, map reading to you is a big bore. They and many other young girls have found the excitement of a new sport called orienteering to be the perfect answer. It combines the challenge of competition with fitness and the enjoyment of nature. It would be ideal for the beginning hikers, before their first expedition but after the fourteen-day training program.

Simply, it is a time race through woods and streams from point to point around an unmarked course. Contestants start individually at intervals, using a topographical map and compass. There are races for novices, and a complete instructional lecture is given by qualified experts in advance on the day of the race, so you need no preparation. Maps are provided for a small entry fee. Usually, compasses can be rented at the registration desk. Most such races take place in the spring and are often organized by a nearby college. Participants are of all ages, and the mood is congenial in a picnic atmosphere, like the gathering of hounds before a fox hunt. Women enjoy the competition because sheer speed or endurance is not the deciding factor. It takes a balance between speed and accuracy because it is a sequence of challenges. Each must be solved correctly while you're moving before you go on to the next. Hasty judgment can mean starting that leg of the race all over again if you become totally disoriented.

It all began as a sport in 1919, when a Swedish Scout leader, Ernest Killander, got the idea for a competition that combined several elements of scouting. Orienteering is now mandatory in Scandinavian public schools. It was popular throughout Europe in the 1930s and came to the United States in 1946, but it has only reached popularity in the 1970s. Orienteers of Wales recently set up the longest course in the history of the game. Contestants ran twenty miles a day for two days. With backpacks and sleeping bags, they checked into campgrounds at night and out at dawn. The Olympic Committee has approved ski orienteering as an Olympic event for 1980. As you might guess, the special appeal to women is a kind of convoluted madness; it is a competitive event that puts the individual on her own against time, using brains and legs; yet it is stimulating and social because of the ambience and the awards.

Information can be obtained from the clubs listed on page 261 or by writing to your state recreation department or to American Orienteering Service, 308 West Fillmore, Colorado Springs, Colorado 80907; or U.S. Orienteering Federation, P.O. Box 1081, Athens, Ohio 45701.

13 | TROUBLE — HOW TO AVOID AND HOW TO DEAL

The line which separates the difficult from the dangerous is sometimes overshadowed, but it is not an imaginary line. It is a true line, without breadth. It is often easy to pass, and very hard to see. It is sometimes passed unconsciously, and the consciousness that it has been passed is felt too late. If the doubtful line is passed consciously, deliberately, one passes from doing that which is justifiable to doing that which is unjustifiable.

—Edward Whymper

The word "trouble" is used now to cover a range of areas where special difficulties may arise for women climbers, from personal health problems to natural threats. There is potential for serious trouble below 15,000 feet even in moderate weather. All of it can be anticipated and avoided, which is why some warnings and directions are included here. It is important to realize that the dangers from high altitude — frostbite, for example — exist only at the extremes. Those potential dangers need not deter you from enjoying the relative safety of the great wilderness world below extreme conditions. Even the extremes up to 30,000 feet have been explored, reported on, and documented so thoroughly in recent years by doctor climbers and scientists that many of the formerly unknown risks are no longer a danger because procedures have been developed to avoid them.

Fatigue

I have noticed that some women are much more easily fatigued than others. Doctors have told me that this is often caused by an iron deficiency. If you believe you become fatigued early and suspect it may be caused by lack of iron, eat foods of high iron content: dark green and deep yellow vegetables (like spinach), cereals, dry beans and molasses. Since some female bodies are less able to utilize the iron than others, it is advisable to take iron pills as well. The woman hiker or climber without fresh foods would be well advised to carry a plastic container of blackstrap molasses for use with cereals, plus iron pills.

Menstruation

Niels H. Lauerssen, M.D., of the New York Hospital–Cornell Medical Center, says in his book *It's Your Body—A Woman's Guide to Gynecology:*

> *If you are leading a terribly active sports life, you may miss one or more of your periods. But don't let this worry you. It just means your releasing hormones are not coming down from the brain. You don't actually have to bleed once a month in order to be healthy. In fact, amenorrhea conserves your iron and may even protect against breast cancer. And your cycle usually starts up again when you take things easier.*

The very experienced women climbers—those I've interviewed, like Irene Miller—say that during the great stress of trying for a peak, they did not menstruate but felt no ill effects during or after. It could be concluded that, like women athletes in track and field who also are at the peak of conditioning and competition and experience amenorrhea, some women climbers who reach altitudes above 10,000 feet and continue on to attempt a summit can expect to skip menstruating temporarily. James E. Crane, M.D., says it is natural that stewardesses and female passengers flying east to west or vice versa at 400 miles per hour or more experience a change in their menstrual cycles when crossing four time zones. The body will take its time to adjust to a new rhythm pattern. So an upset of normal body routine is not to be feared.

Stress

By the time you have reached the 18,000-foot level, you may be well experienced in coping with the stress of expedition life. But, because coping may have been short term, longer and higher climbs may extend you beyond your repertoire of coping responses to the point that illness itself becomes the method of coping. In domestic life, coping behaviors can include smoking, drinking, eating, sex, an outburst of finger-drumming, and nail-biting. Expedition demands will deny these. So, coping resources to deal with the stress of mountain climbing have to be developed. Coping behaviors are basically learned either by observation or by experience. The key word is *learned*.

Dr. Gilbert M. Roberts describes the physiological basis of climbing stress:

Climbing above 18,000 feet (an arbitrary line at best) is hazardous to the health. The physiological stresses imposed on the body in trying to work with less than one-half its usual oxygen supply are considerable. So is the physical discomfort of shortness of breath, nausea, insomnia and migraine-like headaches. There are significant risks of blood clots, strokes, hemorrhage in the retina of the eye (and presumably also in small areas of the brain), frostbite (due not only to cold but also to a decrease in the amount of oxygen available to the body for use in generating heat), exposure and exhaustion. For as yet incompletely understood reasons, high altitude can also lead to serious fluid retention in the brain (cerebral edema), causing coma and even death. It can also cause pulmonary edema—a filling of the small air sacs in the lung with fluid, leading to death from asphyxia—rather like slow drowning. Some climbers who have ventured above 20,000 feet are willing to admit that they returned minus a few I.Q. points and don't think quite as well as they once did. Lack of oxygen also leads to poor coordination and faulty judgment, which in turn can cause accidents and falls that probably wouldn't occur at lower altitudes. Stress resistance is lower, and minor injuries or infection can have much more serious consequences than if they occurred under normal conditions. Little or no acclimatization occurs above 20,000 feet. Generally, the more time you spend at such altitudes, the worse you feel.

The people who do best above 18,000 feet are those between thirty and forty who can pace themselves; who don't panic if they feel less than perfect; and who have excellent kidney function, normal blood pressure, and a high rating on stress tests of cardiac function. They have trimmed excess fat, which uses up oxygen, and have trained hard to stretch heart and lung capacities. Also, they do not smoke. They acclimatize slowly above 10,000 feet—going not more than 2,000 feet a day. They force themselves to cut back on salt intake above 10,000 feet and to drink more water each day (two gallons of fluid per day above 18,000 feet). They take frequent short rest stops—five minutes every hour—and eat frequent snacks of protein and carbohydrates.

Mountain Safety Research of Seattle, Washington, has found by experimenting with climbers on Mount Rainier that those climbers who drink four quarts of fluid a day above 8,000 feet, eat at least three ounces of carbohydrates every hour while climbing, and take enough Rolaids or soda-mint tablets to keep urine at 5.5 to 6.5 pH stay well. (An acidic taste in your mouth will tell you if you need more Rolaids.) If you plan to climb above 10,000 feet, I suggest you read *Mountain Medicine and Physiology*, published in 1975 by the British Alpine Club. If you plan to go to 18,000 feet or more, be sure your expedition has an experienced doctor-climber along.

It is interesting that endurance-type sports, such as marathons and distance swimming, at which women excel (women hold nearly all the distance swimming records, including the two-way swim of the English Channel and the Catalin Channel), are similar to mountain climbing in their physiological demands. These women work close to their maximum level of exertion, as measured by the amount of oxygen consumed, and burns glycogen (stored muscle starch) as a primary fuel. Dietary carbohydrates, when not used immediately by the body, are converted to glycogen and stored in the liver and the muscles. Between meals, the liver glycogen is reconverted to sugar to maintain the blood-glucose level, which is essential to brain activity. The mountain climbers' need for optimum-level brain-functioning activity increases in direct relationship to the number of days out and the altitude gained above the 10,000-foot level. The amount of glycogen that can be stored is finite.

Dr. Ernest Van Aakan, a West German sports physiologist, believes that the female sex hormones, which influence fat accumulation and distribution, may enable women's muscles to utilize fat more readily, but the women climbers will still need sugar to "up" the blood-glucose level for the brain.

In addition to consuming carbohydrates and taking the other physical precautions discussed thus far the high-altitude climber must make psychological adjustments.

Donald L. Dudley, M.D., says:

> People who get along fairly well in life are those who can respond to any given situation with perhaps a dozen different coping behaviors. . . . They can react with anger, sorrow, laughter and logic. They know how to do whatever a given situation calls for. These are the people who can handle a considerable amount of life change. They successfully control their reaction to stressful events and avoid a rise in their blood pressure.

A letter sent out by the National Outdoor Leadership School to a group of climbers preparing to climb Mount McKinley included one line advising them to maintain a "cowlike" nature. The leadership was warning of the fatiguing effects of stress.

> Severe stress can limit or terminate ambition and can provoke tearful emotional collapse or clinical states of shock. Humans have the capacity to endure stress for brief intervals spaced between rehabilitating rests. Response to stress is instinctive, automatic and remarkably efficient. Danger triggers adrenal flow . . . super strength and agility. Emotions, too, peak at extraordinary levels of intensity or seem exquisitely prolonged. Not all of these emotions are primitive or bestial. Stimulation in response to severe stress provokes exalted responses and spiritual transfigurations.

It is in order to control the severity of stress responses and thus avoid the giant "letdown" that the expedition climber must develop a "cowlike" nature in the field. Overreacting is likely to cause the next set of stressful impacts to produce diminished responses and measurably less efficiency—a clear danger to climbing companions.

Weather, too, produces wild swings in human efficiency and moods. A rising barometer makes people cheerful. A falling barometer or rising humidity produces bad moods in people. Monotonous, unchanging weather has a negative effect also. An approaching storm depresses human moods; when it passes, our spirits rise with the rising barometric pressure as the falling humidity produces cool, clear air. Ions in the air affect our moods; negative ions, which are part oxygen, produce a beneficial response in people. Since he has no way of measuring ions without carrying heavy instruments, the mountain climber has to accept their quality, whatever it is. If climbers are already below par in physical condition, the oppressive effects of bad weather can tip the balance. Combined with emotional stress, they may trigger explosive acts of aggression.

The effects of wind and wind-produced noise can cause human beings serious physiological distress. We have little tolerance for wind. Speeds above twenty miles per hour frustrate work or recreation; swirling dust or snow irritates membranes of the nose and throat and causes acute discomfort to the eyes. When human skin is buffeted by strong winds, it transmits distress signals to the brain. We feel uneasy, anxious, even prey to dread. The windstorm outside us can create an intimate response of physical and psychological discomfort.

The noise of a tent flapping or the wind singing through tent ropes, if unabated during a long storm, can be distracting and unnerving to already exhausted climbers. It dulls response to talk, often preventing any conversation that might relieve monotony. Bruce Palmer has produced an interesting book called *Body Weather* which is worth reading. He claims women suffer more than men from the negative effects of wind.

The weather itself will give the expedition climber all the trouble she can handle, and on occasion much more. Naturally, one picks the best season to attempt a climb and goes prepared for the worst. In severe storms you will seldom have more than two choices: to dig in or to retreat. Mountains make wind and weather all their own, so any prediction other than short term by sight and temperature alone is difficult. In the western United States, the prevailing westerly winds, moisture-laden, are forced upward by the mountains in their path. The moisture condenses, to fall as rain or snow. Once clear of the tops, these winds, composed of air that is parched and thin, slide downward. They absorb what little moisture the ground may hold. So, generally, the east side of the mountains has less snow than the west.

Storm clouds are identifiable, and you'll know to expect precipitation when you see one. Recognizing other clouds can help you predict the weather, but mountainous areas often make their own.

Clouds act as insulation, preventing afternoon temperatures from rising to their full potential and keeping overnight readings from dropping rapidly. A sequence of darkening cirrostratus, altostratus and finally nimbostratus over a period of 24 to 48 hours indicates an approaching warm front. Usually, the more extended the sequence, the longer the rain will last. The cloud sequence accompanying a front is faster and more erratic, and often includes thickening altocumulus and stratocumulus, building up to cumulonimbus. A swift wind shift from south to northwest is typical of a passing cold front, with its squall line of clouds, rapidly clearing skies and colder temperatures. A less-pronounced and slower shift from east to south, often preceded by rain, indicates that a warm front has arrived, and a slow improvement and rising temperatures may be anticipated.

Lightning

Lightning strikes the earth about eight million times every day. Strikes in the United States alone kill some 150 persons each year. From 1960 to 1971, the American Alpine Club recorded seven lightning accidents on U.S. mountains. Seventeen people were involved; seven were killed. That's fewer than one climber a year, but since mountaintops are likely to receive strikes, a few details may be valuable to you.

Lightning is an electrical discharge—an enormous spark. It occurs mainly in towering cumulonimbus clouds, or thunderclouds, which are characterized by strong updrafts and downdrafts, with velocities that are commonly from 10 to 30 miles per hour but have been known to exceed 100 miles per hour. A thunderstorm may have a diameter of 1 to 2 kilometers and an altitude of 6 to 8 kilometers from cloud base to cloud top.

You can estimate the distance to a lightning flash by counting the seconds from the time you see the flash until you hear the thunder. For every second, count about 1,000 feet. For example, if it takes five seconds for the thunder to reach you, the lightning is a mile away. If the lightning is so close that you cannot hear the thunder, you are a part of the strike!

In a storm, stay away from peaks and ridges; they will get the strikes first. Avoid steep inclines. Find a flat ledge or a gentle slope. If possible, stay near a pinnacle that can act as a lightning rod. Position yourself at a distance from the base, but not at a greater distance than the height of the pinnacle itself. Crouch low, touching the ground only with soles of your boots; or sit on insulating material such as coiled climbing rope. Avoid caves or overhanging ledges. They have proved worthless as shelter from lightning strikes.

Snakes

Fear of snakes, especially the "rattler," is the result of ignorance, baseless fables and myth. The sure cure for fear is to apply a large dose of knowledge. The definitive source for this treatment is Laurence M. Klauber's *Rattlesnakes: Their Habits, Life Histories and Influence on Mankind*, consisting of two volumes and published by the University of California Press in 1956. The price is $22.50, so no doubt you'll want to borrow it from the public library.

Meanwhile, I can tell you with certainty two facts: First, the venom is deadly poisonous but not fatal if you act quickly. Second, avoiding rattlesnake bites is as easy as avoiding typhoid, food poisoning, etc. I only wish as much were known about cancer as about snakes.

You need to be concerned only if you are going into an area at a time when snakes are known to be a threat. Check with local authorities just as you would to avoid Montezuma's Revenge from water or food. If your investigation indicates caution, carry first aid treatment for all persons in your party. In advance, teach your companions how to avoid snakebite, and instruct them in treatment procedures. In this way you relieve the anxiety and ignorance that might cause the victim and/or her companions to panic when a bite occurs.

Two treatments are recommended; carry both in your kit. "Cut and suck" originated long before the 1940s cowboy movie that showed the hero getting conveniently bitten on the forearm, so that with the other hand he could whip out his sheath knife and in perfect macho fashion cut a line between the fang marks and suck out the poison and bad blood with his own mouth. If he'd gotten bit on the foot or lower leg, where 99 percent of snakebites occur, he would have looked ridiculous and unheroic on the silver screen with his foot in his mouth. No doubt he was crawling on his hands and knees, sneaking up on an Indian village to rescue the captured maiden. Anyway, the method still works, but as a convenience (so you won't have to put your foot in your mouth or somebody else's), the Cutter Compak Suction Kit, pocket size, with scientific instructions, is available for under $3 at sporting goods stores where hunting and fishing gear is sold.

The other treatment is called cryotherapy. It works by cooling the bitten area to such a degree that the body will absorb the venom slowly enough to neutralize its most serious effects. For use in the field, doctors recommend carrying ethyl chloride, which evaporates quickly when applied to the skin and cools the immediate area. My action would be to apply the suction cups and the cooling process simultaneously.

(It should be obvious that one should not suck with the mouth and apply ethyl chloride simultaneously.)

In my time in the field, which included the Everglades, the Georgia swamps, and the desert country of the Southwest, I have not been bitten nor have any of my companions. In fact, in talking with cowboys and rangers over the years, I have never met anyone who has been bitten. So I feel a little silly discussing snakes as though they were a likely source of trouble to the hiker. Ross Allen of Ocala, Florida, a great snake expert until his death (not by snakebite), and Bill Hass of the Miami Serpentarium, both of whom I interviewed and photographed with their snakes over a period of years, provided the only firsthand experience and expert secondhand knowledge.

All of us, women in particular, have an inborn dread of reptiles that is exaggerated beyond all reality. In *The Dragons of Eden,* Carl Sagan says:

> [Sherman] Washburn has reported that infant baboons and other young primates appear to be born with only three inborn fears: falling, snakes, and the dark.
>
> Since, according to Washburn, young primates exhibit an inbred fear of snakes, it is easy to wonder whether the dream world does not point directly as well as indirectly to the ancient hostility between reptiles and mammals.

The answer to this fear is knowledge. Books written by experts, coupled with firsthand observation of snakes in captivity in zoos or on snake farms, can counteract the natural physiological threat. Observe the various types and learn to recognize the dangerous variety. You will be able to evaluate with your own intelligence the rattler's threat. Rattlesnakes are neither quick moving, aggressive, nor cunning; handlers can walk among them without being attacked.

Therefore, you can conclude that the only dangerous rattler is the one you don't see. You may see some in captivity that are six or eight feet in size. In the wild, the largest of the thirty other species—the eastern diamondback—will be three to four feet long.

You should know, too, that their vision is poor and they cannot hear. They can smell (with the flicking of their forked tongues). They are sensitive to heat and vibrations. Avoid night movement if possible; when it is necessary, walk heavily. Snakes are cold blooded; and their bodies maintain the temperature of the ground they crawl on. Cold puts them into hibernation. They seldom prowl at a temperature lower than 65°F. They hardly move at 45°F. They are most active at 80–90°F; at 100° they are suffering; and at 110° they will die of heat stroke. Keep in mind that those temperatures are rattlesnake temperatures, not the weather bureau's figures. If the official temperature is 60° (taken at a height of 5 feet in the shade), the snake may be basking in direct sunlight between rocks. When the air temperature is 80° in the desert, the ground or sand in the sun may be at 110°.

In warm weather rattlesnakes forage for food two hours before sunset. If during that time the ground temperature is between 80° and 90°, watch sharply. When the ground temperature is near 100° in the sun, you know that shaded areas present your only danger. If the sun is shining but a cold wind is blowing, rattlesnakes will keep to sunlit areas that are sheltered from the wind.

Bears

Wild bears (nonpark bears) such as those native to Alaska are the safest kind. In the United States, the grizzly is wild only in remote areas of Montana, Idaho and Wyoming. In those areas, you should remember that in the summertime wild bears usually have lots of food without having to attack people. And in the winter they are hibernating.

After considerable research, Janet Hopson of *Outside Magazine* suggests the following to avoid grizzly danger:

Do not bring along perfume or cosmetics.

Do not bring your dog.

Do not hike alone, sleep alone without a tent, or menstruate!

Do keep campsite, tents, backpacks free of food and food odors.

Do make noise at all times when hiking; avoid carrion; store food, soap and garbage high in a tree at least 200 feet from camp.

If you see a grizzly, cross upward at a distance of 200 to 300 feet so the bear can smell you, and make noise. Constantly watch the bear's movements. If it is approaching from a distance, climb a high tree. If it approaches from nearby, stand still or quietly withdraw. If it charges, drop back to distract or delay the bear, and run for a tree. If you are trapped short, drop to the ground before the bear reaches you and play dead, lying face down with your legs together and hands clasped behind your neck. Don't cry out or struggle.

Park bears are a different matter entirely. They have been conditioned by humans and act very differently from wild bears.

At the turn of the century, when the national parks were building hotels and lodges, it was discovered by accident that bears like garbage. So delighted were the tourists to get this easy look at the wild bears that bleachers were constructed and floodlights installed on the sites without a thought for the consequences. The use of open dumps was not discontinued in Yosemite until 1970. By then, through several generations, black bears had become dependent on the food of civilized humans. (Once again, a taste of our life-style has been a destructive force—as our liquor was to the red man, and our snowmobile to the Eskimo.)

Unfortunately, lack of foresight on the part of park management was not the sole cause of this condition. The eager tourist clutching her Brownie or Polaroid tried to feed the cute cubs from the safety of her car. In 1975, visitors, jaws agape, watched bears in the act of "car clouting." A 300- to 500-pound adult bear can run 35 miles per hour, tear five-inch limbs from trees, "peel a car door open like an overripe banana or bite off a chunk of convertible top, or break out a window with a powerful forearm. It reaches or crawls inside, sniffs and paws the upholstery, then looks for the exposed food that drew its attention in the first place."

The public are the guilty ones. Says one ranger, "A lot of them are secretly thrilled when a bear rips them off. It makes their trip."

The most recent trick of the cunning black bears is the bluff. They have learned that backpacks contain food. They pretend to charge the hikers, who drop their packs to run. And the bears' bluff is rewarded. Cliff Martinka, bear biologist in Glacier Park, says, "The bears here seem to have gotten a new message. Humans aren't to be feared as natural enemies." In Glacier Park in 1976 there was a fatal mauling. Three people were injured by grizzlies, and black bears began charging hikers. Park Service statistics report that in 1977 there were eight black bear attacks in

Great Smoky; six attacks in Yosemite; four in Sequoia-Kings Canyon; and three in the Grand Tetons. (No fatalities were reported.)

Janet Hopson's advice on meeting black bears in a national park is: "Cache your food in accordance with park rules. If a bear comes after your pack, don't yell, throw things, or run! Retreat quietly from campsite if food is properly stored. It you are cooking, and food plates and garbage are exposed, carry them with you as you leave. If the bear threatens you directly by charging, woofing or snapping its jaws, give it what it demands, and report the incident as quickly as possible."

My advice is to avoid national parks except in the winter unless you're with a group. Learn to distinguish between black bears and grizzlies. Glacier Park poses the most dangerous threat from bears. In the spring and summer, a hiker or climber should camp with a group of four to six people and with two to three tents. Obviously, hanging on a mountainside is the safest place to be.

Falling Rocks and Avalanches

Falling rocks and avalanches of snow or ice are natural hazards of which even the beginner needs to be aware. In planning a climb or talking with natives in a new climbing area, one should seek information about any specific patterns of weather or temperature that might precipitate a fall. Wearing a helmet in a suspect rock area is just common sense. A blow to an unprotected head from even a small stone could be disastrous. Some mountains, by geographic formation weathering, are prone to stone fall. Ice or snow melts during the day, and the water penetrates the cracks; at night it freezes again and expands, dislodging the loosened rock.

One doesn't hear or read much about the danger of falling stone or rock. I rather suspect this is because it's never a whole landslide—just the mountain pushing off in one or two places—and the odds, out of all that mountain space, that one piece will hit one climber are very small. If one does get hit, the odds are great that his companions will never know it was a rock; only that their climbing companion fell off the mountain; thankful that he did not pull them off too. The shock of a fall may be so great that the climber, scrambling on rope to right himself, is more interested in recovery and a new foothold than in analysis. He'll no doubt be bruised in several places, and he won't have time to think about which fell first, the rock or his body.

Helmets are expensive, but if a climb is important, and you have determined from several sources that there is clear and present danger from your anticipated climb, either buy or rent one. Use a bicycle type if nothing else. Helmets must fit well, not rattle around. But don't miss the climb because that mountain face has a reputation for falling rock; just give yourself the comfort of protection, because it's like bad weather. If you're in the middle of a climb, there is little you can do to protect yourself if you didn't have the forethought to bring that protection with you. I believe the best helmets are made and sold by Mountain Safety Research, South 96th Street at 8th Avenue South, Seattle, Washington 98108.

In the heat of the day is the most dangerous time to climb a steep rock face. By the same reasoning, north-face climbs are generally less provocative of falling stone.

For the active rock climber, falls are inevitable; but with judicious use of rope, hammer and hardware, and in the company of competent climbers, she can avoid serious falls. Even a fall on a well-anchored short rope can produce trouble. Some climbers use a waist coil instead of a diaper sling, just wrapping the rope around the waist for quick rappelling. Even though such a coil can break a fall, it can be risky, because all of the climber's weight is caught at one point. Paralysis of the diaphragm and death by suffocation can occur in twenty-two minutes—ten minutes in which to save yourself and twelve minutes to finish dying if you fail. Mountain Safety Research makes a five-point harness that supports the upper body as well as the lower, but it is no good for women for the reason that it puts pressure on the breasts and is too narrow in the crotch. Work is currently being done on a special design to accommodate the female anatomy.

Snow and ice avalanches are another story. If there seems to be clear and present danger, don't climb; find another route. Cornices are a risk for the climber, whether he or she is on or below them. Snow avalanches are more of a hazard in winter than in summer, and are fatal if the climber is trapped in one. One would do well to make a careful study of the area before joining a winter climb. Advance knowledge of the conditions that produce avalanches will assure more restful nights on the mountainside. During a January climb of the Grand Tetons, in risky areas we climbed 25 to 30 feet apart, each of us trailing a bright red avalanche cord (20 feet long) tied around his waist to enable the survivors to find those who might be buried. "To survive burial, one must quickly thrash his arms up by his face to open a breathing space in the snow. Some climbers have been found alive two

hours after burial," advised my climbing companion,
Rick Palaster. Fear and those words drove me to
exhaustive reading and study before my next winter
climb. Discussion with experienced climbers is much
more informative and productive than mere library
reading.

Snow avalanches can be aggravated by the weight
of a skier or climber, by additional snowfall, or by
rising temperatures. Rain, too, adds weight. On a
snowy or winter climb, be sure your leader has a thor-
ough knowledge of possible avalanches in the area
you will be climbing; better still, become your own
investigating expert. Be aware that the center of an
avalanche moves faster than the outer edges. If you
should see one starting farther up the mountainside,
don't take for granted that you will be safe because
you are on a ridge. Ice is a viscous substance much
like dough and can fill depressions or rise over hills.
Melting ice and water beneath it lubricate its path. If
you should find yourself directly on its course, consider not only retreating directly backwards up a hill,
but also getting to the side of the avalanche.

If you should become trapped in an avalanche, the
odds are that you won't survive. However, Matthias
Zdarsky, a skier, did. He received eighty separate
fractures and dislocations during the few minutes it
took to happen, and was fully conscious through it all.
When it was over, he was lying uncovered on the surface of the snow. It took eleven years for rehabilita-
tion, but he lived to ski again.

Axe Safety

You have learned how to use a sharp knife safely in
the kitchen, as the result of direction and practice

over several years. If you have not had advance practice or direction, using an axe can be dangerous. A
long-handled one is safest for a beginner to use, because if you miss a log or branch lying on the ground,
the arc of your swing will carry the head of the axe
into the ground, not into your leg or foot. A short-
handled axe is less cumbersome to carry because it is
less bulky and weighs less. To safely use an axe with a
short handle to cut branches lying on the ground,
squat down with your left knee on the ground if
you're right-handed, right knee if you're left-handed.
In this way you are close to the ground, and the arc of
your swing will end with the blade in the ground if
you miss. When you use any strange tool for the first
time, take the time to experiment, observe, and examine. Is the head loose or tight? After a few light blows,
can you determine if the blade is sharp? Touch the
edge with your finger to learn to gauge sharpness and
nicks. Are you able to grip the handle tightly? Does it
feel secure when you take a full swing? Gloves may
give you a better grip as well as protection from splin-
ters when handling wood. A dull axe, hitting hard at
an angle, may glance or bounce off, causing you
momentary loss of control. Without swinging full
strength, test the angle at which you want to cut to see
whether the axe will penetrate the wood or bounce
off. You should carry a sharpening file to use when
needed. To trim limbs off a trunk, always put the
trunk between you and the limb you are cutting.
Work in a clean space without stones. Do not brace or
lean a limb against another log or stone, as it might fly
up and hit you when it snaps on impact. It is better to
lay the limb flat on clear ground and hold it in position with your foot. Obviously, your foot should be a
safe distance from the target, and your swing should

be controlled. Wear sunglasses and hard-toed shoes for additional protection.

When not using the axe, lay it flat on the ground; in any other position it could be dangerous. When carrying it on your back or by hand, enclose the blade in a protective case. When carrying it a short distance between cutting areas, hold it by the handle in one hand near the blade, with the cutting edge down.

An *ice axe* is a much needed, valuable tool for climbing in snow and ice at high altitude. It is used in many ways, such as for cutting steps and for self-arrest. When you have reached that stage of usage, take the time to research the best tool. Mountain Safety Research has done considerable testing. Ice axes with wooden handles are outdated and unsafe.

Acute Mountain Sickness

Acute mountain sickness can cause serious trouble. It is an illness caused by high altitude, and is characterized by shortness of breath, fatigue, general debility, and often nausea. It may strike any time from a few hours to a few days after ascending, and occurs most commonly above 12,000 feet. It rarely attacks a healthy person at an altitude below 8,200 feet. Avoiding physiological stress is the best prevention.

Frostbite and Hypothermia

Two illnesses caused by extreme cold are frostbite—in which ice crystals form between the cells—and hypothermia—where the body temperature cools to the point of inpairment of vital functions. However, neither of these is caused by cold alone; fatigue, hunger and dehydration are major factors in bringing them about.

Frostbite begins as a sharp pain that turns to numbness. Skin color is pale in minor cases; it becomes blue and hard when frostbite is severe. Treat it by warming the area, preferably with body heat. Never rub, exercise, or put snow on it.

Symptoms of hypothermia include shivering, fatigue, a feeling of deep cold, a loss of coordination, and blueness or puffiness of the skin. The victim should be kept dry and sheltered. Warm her by either putting her into a sleeping bag with another person, giving her hot drinks, or immersing her in a tub of hot water.

To sum up, remember that climbers who are least troubled by acute mountain sickness (AMS), high altitude pulmonary edema (HAPE), hypothermia (HY), and frostbite (FB) are those who are: (1) good-natured and avoid stress; (2) sensitive to "body talk"; (3) free of circulation problems in lower limbs; and (4) well conditioned from training between climbs.

Lost!

You are never lost to this planet until you stop breathing. (Even then you may not be lost in spirit or soul to other worlds. No one has proved total termination!)

Temporary indecision about which direction to follow or how long it will take to return to base camp or a roadhead does not mean one is "lost." If you got from A to B in the first place, you can get from B to A—even if you haven't yet learned how to subconsciously mark your route. Noting sun direction, time of travel, and landmarks is good training. You have been moving over ground at your own pace with your eyes open, I hope; so if you take the time to calculate calmly and *believe* you are not lost, you will eventually be able to reconstruct your path.

Most likely you have had the experience of trying to find a certain place late at night, with no choice but to continue searching until familiar landmarks or simple logic brought you there. You were delayed and confused, but felt in no great danger, knowing that at worst you could lock your car and wait for daylight. You felt secure in the knowledge that the road would be traveled the next day. The difference in the wilderness is that you don't have that "next day" security. However, if you're confident about your survival ability, you will solve the problem alone.

To reconstruct your progress, start with your last direction change and work backwards one stage at a time. Try to make several verifications of each change: landmarks, sun direction on the compass, and time. Don't hesitate to shout and blow your whistle every hour or so. Reconcile yourself to the fact that you aren't going to catch the next train. It will be up to you; accept the time it will take. Elements permitting, you can survive for an unlimited time.

If this happens at night and you can't see the stars to navigate or find a path to walk, it is best to stay put until daylight; that is, if you can find shelter from the elements. One exception would be in the winter in snow, when even at night you could still see your footprints or ski tracks by which to return—fortunate for you, since you might freeze without proper shelter.

On a mountaintop, because of the strain of fatigue and rare air, a retreat to a lower level—even if it is nighttime or foggy—would be the best action, despite uncertainty of location.

Finally, to prevent confusion and the inconvenience of walking in ever-widening circles, remember the following advice: Have a topical map and know how to use it. From the time you start out, mark your progress every night. Do not for any reason separate yourself from your group without having a companion with you. And carry your compass, map, matches and whistle on your person, not in your pack.

Pain and Injuries

Following are some common complaints that you may be able to avoid—or cure early—if you are aware of them. They can occur both in training and while actually hiking and climbing.

Most foot and leg problems result from lack of stretching. Make it a habit to take time to stretch and massage your legs several times a day, whether on the trail or running. If you become conscious of a feeling of tightness in the muscles, take time to stretch and relax before pain or soreness develops.

BLISTERS are probably the most common injury you will have to deal with while hiking or running. Before going out, check the insides of your running shoes or boots for any rough spots. Do not wear socks with holes.

Blisters are best treated by making a small hole in each blister with a sterile needle and allowing the fluid to drain. The skin under it has to dry, so cover blisters only when hiking or running. Otherwise, try to keep them exposed to the air. The use of thicker socks may prevent recurrence of the blisters. Some runners use

Vaseline either to cover the feet completely or to coat just the bad spots. Also, using tape or pads will help.

CALLUSES are generally caused by wearing street shoes that are too large, or by wearing wooden clogs or odd-shaped sandals. To remove calluses, rub with pumice stone while in the bathtub until the callus feels smooth.

ARCH PAIN. Most boots come with good built-in arch supports, but sneakers and jogging shoes sometimes lack this support. If you feel pain in the arches, try inserting a Dr. Scholl's arch support No. 10.

BLACK TOE is so-called because the big toenail turns black or blue; sometimes it disintegrates and falls off. There is usually no pain. It is caused by the toe jamming up against the boot or sneaker, which either may be too short or may not be laced tightly enough. The nail will take months to grow back, so try to avoid shoes or boots that are too short. A shoemaker can sometimes stretch your boots or shoes.

HEEL PAIN is caused by pressure on the heel bone itself, which is protected by the soft tissue of the heel bottom. If the tissue is weak or thin, the bone will either develop "spurs" or become bruised. To treat, get a "heel cup," which is a small plastic support for the heel that pushes the tissue under the heel and itself adds a cushioning. Heel cups are sold at sports shops or at YMCA shops and are inexpensive. The heel hits the ground three times harder in running than in walking. It is a good idea to use heel cups whenever jogging on the streets.

SORE RIDGE is an area above the arch where the bone touches the tongue and laces. It can sometimes become painful from continuous pressure. You'll have to skip some lace holes in that area to cure it when wearing running shoes. With boots, you'll have to add a soft pad of thin foam rubber the length of the tongue inside the boot. You may have to tape it over your socks to keep it in position on the trail.

ACHILLES TENDINITIS is a swelling of the tendon below the calf muscle. It is usually caused by a tightening in the calf muscles from overwork or by improper stretching and loosening-up exercises. For relief, apply ice packs, or plunge up to your knee in a cold stream or lake. If you are out in the field, shorten your stride, and try climbing hills backwards or sideways.

SHIN SPLINTS is injury to or inflammation of the shin area of the leg. It is usually caused by running or walking on hard surfaces or by unequal development of the lower leg muscles. It hurts worst when you are going downhill. To avoid this, wear running shoes with a good cushioned sole. To relieve pain, use ice packs, or plunge your legs in a cold stream.

SCIATICA is pressure on the sciatic nerve, which runs through the pelvis and into the upper leg. This pressure can produce a variety of symptoms, with pain in the lower back and hips being the most common. Sometimes it also produces a numbness in the feet or toes. The cause can be varied, but to prevent or relieve it, the best exercises are bent-knee sit-ups to strengthen the abdominal muscles and stretching exercises for the hamstrings.

14 | EXPEDITION BEHAVIOR AND LEADERSHIP

The lessons learned on the playing field are among the most basic: the setting of goals and joining with others to achieve them; an understanding of and respect for rules; the persistence to hone ability into skill, prowess into perfection.
—B. J. Phillips

Behavior of a woman hiker, whether she's with male or female companions, will generally vary greatly, depending on whether she originated the expedition or accepted another's invitation to join. In the one case you put yourself in a leadership role and therefore have certain responsibilities to the other member or members of the group. As a beginner, your role is usually that of a follower. But whether you are a leader or a follower, it's crucial to remember that your behavior, your ability to get along with the other members of your expedition, is a key element in the success of your trip.

In his book *Wilderness Handbook*, Paul Petzoldt states:

Human nature influences the success or failure, comfort or discomfort, safety or danger of an outdoor experience as much as equipment, logistics, trail techniques, rations and other basic organizational concerns. Although a breakdown

176

in personal relations between individuals is encouraged by poor planning, even the well-thought-out and well-equipped outing might face failure, injury or death if good expedition behavior practices are missing. In high altitudes or during adventuresome, energy-draining endeavors, outdoorspeople must make a concerted effort for the consideration of companions in addition to securing their own personal comfort and safety.

Many climbing trips and expeditions sponsored by clubs, societies, or nations select participants on the basis of competitions, daring exploits, and extraordinary feats of skill or endurance. Often, such outdoor "prima donnas" care only about fame, reaching the summit, being first and are unconcerned that their personal success may be attained at the expense of the enjoyment, companionship and even safety of others.

He goes on to describe several expeditions that ended tragically when proper expedition behavior was missing:

The attempt to plant a United States flag atop Mount Everest in 1971 was a classic example. Thirty-two persons representing eleven countries and speaking eight different languages led an army of four hundred low altitude porters and forty-two Sherpas to the highest mountain in the world. Renowned climbers from the United States, Great Britain, Switzerland, France, Italy, Norway, Japan, Austria and India were brought together for the assault.

Because it was deemed impractical to accommodate so many varied national diets in the rations allotment, it was decided to compromise by purchasing central European food. But no one realized that the Austrian appointed to be in charge of commissary was a vegetarian and health food faddist. His five tons of supplies included a venison substitute made of chopped nuts, dried fruit bars, a Swiss herb and yeast "Biostreth Elixir," sauerkraut, pickled cucumbers, and·

five hundred family-sized tins of whole meal pumpernickel (which he was the only one to even taste). The remainder of the party grumbled over meals and suffered from inadequate nutrition.

A French political hopeful, an Italian and a Swiss woman were bent on becoming the first Frenchman, Italian and woman on top of Everest. However, when progress was slowed down to the extent of their being asked to assist the Sherpas in carrying supplies to the upper camps, they claimed insult to their native countries and abandoned the expedition. The leader attempted to coax them back, but the woman responded by pelting him with rocks and snowballs.

Death struck an Indian representative of the party when he attempted a difficult rope traverse during a storm. He was moving to a lower camp with the Austrian commissary chairman. The Austrian negotiated the tricky ledge, but when his companion did not appear behind him after twenty minutes, he returned to camp and sent rescuers. No one was able to reach the victim. His body dangled from ropes for six days before it could be retrieved. The Indian had been too proud to admit that he had had no previous experience with such a rope traverse and delayed calling for help until it was too late.

Someone broke out a bottle of whiskey in hopes of relieving growing tension; this only provided a catalyst for a monumental row with invectives shouted in four languages. The entire undertaking was tragic and unhappy because Expedition Behavior skills were lacking. (For a detailed description of the 1971 Everest assault see "Ordeal on Everest," by Murray Sayle, in Life, *July 2, 1971.)*

Annapurna, *a book by Maurice Herzog, honestly describes a negative situation. Members of the party not only had trouble getting along under normal circumstances, they hated one another when their mountaineering abilities failed to match the demands of their mission. Ailing companions were deserted, and some persons were so affected by high altitudes and emotional pressure that they completely lost their judgment.*

Such conflicts are much more common than the reader of articles and published journals would suspect, since incidents that might cast doubt on the stability or unselfishness of members are generally omitted from post-mortem accounts. Traditionally, it has not been "good form" to admit that such situations occur. Scores of mountaineering books close by depicting the expeditioners returning to civilization with life-long friendships cemented by the trip.

The longer the trip or harder the circumstances, the greater the strain on individuals, but one must not neglect expedition behavior basics on any trek. These matters affect and concern the weekend hiker as well as the Everest climber.

Food, comfort (clothes and shelter), physical resources (energy and time)—these are factors affecting a hiker's disposition and personality in joint living situations that must be taken into consideration when planning out each day of the expedition. Trouble with our bodies affects our head.

Observing the following basic guidelines is as much a personal responsibility of the individual hiker as of the leadership: Eat often on the trail to maintain body warmth and energy. Regulate body functions by taking vitamin C, eating fresh fruits, supplying salt needs, and drinking continually (to avoid dehydration and irritability). Choose clothes and tents wisely to assure the greatest possible degree of personal comfort. Conserve energy resources to prevent extreme fatigue. Of course, the leadership must be wise in planning the group's time so schedules and goals can be realized without strain and anxiety, outside of what weather or accidents might cause. If a group is comfortable and relaxed and conditions are ideal, you can expect the best of human nature.

Trouble with human nature can be expected when accidents happen, clothes are lost, food spoils or runs

low, feet and hands get cold. People without experience and conscious control can become animals. The
metamorphosis is often shockingly sudden.

Failure to maintain good behavior is a failure in
human relations. Causes include indifference to
others, lack of introspection, poor communication,
lack of understanding, ignorance, personality faults,
rationalization of responsibility, inability or unwill-
ingness to accept blame, selfishness, and—worst and
rarest—either cowardice or inability to identify survival of other members of your team with your own.

Good expedition behavior requires a sensitive
awareness of leadership, individual hikers, tentmates,
and the authorities who govern or supervise a region
you are in. Most important of all are the intangible
personality traits of spirit and motivation that infuse
the group with a feeling of purpose, friendship and
concern for others. As Tartanion put it in *The Three
Musketeers:* "One for all and all for one."

Keeping a contented, involved group is everybody's
problem—not just the leader's. A woman's behavior
on an expedition with men has a special significance
because of the way most men react to women. If she
has an attractive personality or good looks, she can
help group male behavior by not demonstrating any
particular alliance with any one man—better to mix
with all. And women should avoid forming little
cliques of "women only" for social time, for there are
likely to be sensitive or shy males in any group. These
rules work in reverse just as well—men too should
spend social time with and give personal contact to all
group members so each has an equal feeling of
recognition.

Almost every act or word within a small, tight

group can have significance. The habit of reflecting before acting is worth developing. I remember very well a time I spent in the Wind River Mountains of Wyoming with a large mixed group. There was no overall objective to reach a certain peak. It was a casual expedition composed of strangers, and the leader was an expert. He had the attention and respect of all members of the group for eight days. On the ninth day, after some rappelling and rock-climbing instruction, he chose one woman to climb with him in the afternoon. Their little afternoon excursion did not start a flaming affair, but the rest of the climbers were left to their own devices and the appearance of favoritism affected them. I witnessed former admirers turning sour and backbiting by the end of the trip. Of course, such reactions are immature. However, leaders should be aware of the limitations of human nature and try to anticipate the consequences of their actions.

On most co-ed expeditions, even today, women have the option of taking or leaving responsibilities—i.e., they can leave chores, navigation, cooking, etc., to male companions, most of whom will accept that situation without resentment, or they can try to share equally as they would have to with an all-woman group. Irene Miller, a California climber, told me she found that she had to assert herself forcefully with male climbers who were perfectly content to "carry" her. It's not necessarily that men are aggressive about leadership roles—they have been taught to take care of women. Some men have not changed to a sexless, impartial, objective attitude toward women. Most modern women understand this and deal with co-ed trips either by accepting men's limitations or by charting chores and roles in advance in order to maintain good behavior relationships throughout an expedition. It is certainly a matter for discussion between the men and women on even a weekend hike. Irene Miller pointed out to me that climbing with men has that "pleasure-pain" conflict. "It's comfortable with a man because he's not going to demand, expect, or push you. It is only with an all-woman team that you are really being counted on for your share."

I think it's important on an expedition with a large group of strangers that an individual become acquainted with everyone else in the group. Even a short conversation will give each a reading on the other that not only creates a congenial atmosphere but sets up a familiar basis for cooperation in case of an emergency in the future. It is not necessary to keep a dossier or take notes, but be aware of people and their performance. Awareness is the first step in learning to judge characters and ability.

It is good practice to appraise yourself honestly before you embark on the "encounter-like" experience of an expedition in the wilderness. Your idiosyncrasies are certainly evident to you if you've had roommates or lived with others in your family. You may have to adjust some of your own personal traits to avoid annoying a group. The advance introspection should be constructive rather than negative. Figure out how you can avoid, control or substitute in situations that might lead to unpleasant reactions by others. Most importantly, just resolve that you are young enough (in heart), strong enough (in will), and willing enough (in spirit) to recognize and to adopt whatever behaviors are necessary to deal successfully with human nature. A little humbleness expressed to any "offended souls" usually wipes out old scars.

The one-to-one relationship between you and your tentmate is probably the most personal one you'll encounter on any outing. There is an intimacy in sharing that tiny pyramid enclosure with someone else that requires a degree of tolerance one seldom experiences in city life. Having two people in a tent—even if it is a three-man tent—will avoid the possibility of the three-way triangle developing. With three in a tent, one person is apt to feel left out or disapproved of, because the chemistry of all three will never mesh equally.

It's best for the expedition if each member tents with a stranger rather than a friend. This puts everyone on the same basis and prevents the feeling of dislocation that develops when friendship cliques are evident. It is also a good idea to mix people from different environmental backgrounds—especially if the hikers are young. Meeting and sharing with new friends both enhance enjoyment and create an atmosphere in which each person is trying to make himself or herself more acceptable to the other. You may recall having witnessed the charm of a younger brother or sister in a social situation and having thought that "this is not the same snot-nosed kid who is always so rude to me." It is in human nature to put one's best face forward in beginnings.

Mixing people of the same relative age, boys with girls, often produces the best results. The presence of members of the opposite sex can inspire exemplary behavior.

Tentmates share equally the chores of pitching the tent, cooking and cleaning up. Inside the tent, the choice of sleeping-bag side should be by agreement or rotation. Once your tentmate has unpacked her bag, you should avoid putting any of your articles or yourself on her side. Try, within reason, to respect the other person's territory.

In Chapter 10 I mentioned the advantages of working out a privacy schedule so each tentmate has time inside alone. Your side of the tent should be neatly arranged, with dirty clothes, socks, etc., out of sight if you're not inside. Tools, cooking items, and such should be placed in a mutually-agreed-upon storage space near packs that are kept outside. That way you will avoid accidents and you will both know where to look for shared equipment. Using or moving or losing someone else's personal items is a quick way to develop resentment. Every item a person has on a hike is valuable to her for comfort and often safety, so you spoil a balance by assuming a privilege.

Consideration is the key. If you show great concern for the others' comfort and possessions they are very likely to return the favor.

It is unfair to the group if your dress is raunchy and reeky; men especially have the problem of thinking outdoor wilderness means that dirty is "in." Because we are bred and raised in a visual world where appearance is something we are all aware of, it is poor behavior to allow oneself to degenerate to the state of being an eyesore. Personal cleanliness is difficult out of doors—bathing in the icy water of mountain streams can be painful. But a practical attempt should be made to clean at least your face and hands. Just combing your hair can present a better picture. Smelly, spotted, dirty clothes are inevitable on a long trip, but you should make an effort to clean them or change when possible.

General neatness and order can be more important in camp than at home. Dirty dishes mean flies. Gear and tools carelessly tossed aside can mean loss or damage that might affect the entire party.

It is often in the division of food that conflicts and irritation arise. Leaders generally find it best to distribute food to groups of four who cook together. Everybody doesn't eat the same quantities or even have the same needs. Those who are young and slender may need a larger share of the carbohydrates than others, but everyone should feel free to eat whatever amount he or she wants at mealtimes. Stealing or hoarding food from the general food supply can cause bitter resentments and is a clear sign of an individual's fears and weaknesses—a fundamental indication to a leader that that person could be dangerous to the group in an emergency situation!

There are certain dangers in any extended trip in a wilderness area. In reality such an excursion is probably no more dangerous than highway driving or city life, but isolation from medical facilities and the convenience of vehicular speed does make the threat seem more real. Practical jokes, horseplay, and the reckless daredevil cannot be tolerated because of the serious consequences that might result from accidents in a remote area. Experienced leaders can tell you of the destruction to a group's enjoyment caused by a burn, break or cut that required an emergency evacuation. Individuals must learn to anticipate the consequences of their actions and control their desires in order to ensure the welfare of the majority. If your leader tells you that gloves are supplied for cooking to prevent burned fingers over an open fire and you ignore those directions and burn your hand, you will not be any help holding a rope for a belay the next day. The group suffers because of your personal whim. If you're told to wear your boots to cross a stream and you cross barefooted instead and cut your feet, somebody else is going to have to carry your pack; you may even have to be evacuated.

One preeminent maxim of expedition behavior is never to leave your group unless you are sent out for a purpose with your leader's approval. A good leader would usually send two people together anyway. It is a mistake to be alone in the wilderness if it can be avoided.

It may seem to you almost silly to discuss behavior in such detailed terms when common sense would seem to cover most of the possibilities. But for common sense to be of value other than in retrospect, the facts and environment have to be common. If you have never been on an expedition in wilderness, it is an uncommon situation, and thinking about it in advance can help to clarify ideas and make correct behavior a more natural reaction.

When you join a group, it is implied that you accept them all—strong and weak. Even humorous ridicule of a person's minor misfortune can be a destructive act. Belittling someone who is slower can come back to haunt you. There should be an atmosphere of kindly commitment to companions, especially the least skilled or slowest. The stronger should share the loads of the weaker in a friendly, willing manner. You should think of your group as a family unit in which the older or stronger assist and feel responsible for the younger or weaker. If you are barely holding your own and cannot practically lend a hand, at least lend some spirit and good wishes—a word of encouragement.

The only danger of being a good follower is that

one grows comfortable in that role. Every woman interested in hiking and climbing should be motivated to gain the complete all-round experience and knowledge required to assume leadership. Unfortunately, nowadays it is difficult for a woman to obtain a leadership role in a co-ed climb unless she has exceptional qualities and a great deal of knowledge. The best way to gain such knowledge is to begin as a good follower on co-ed climbs and then to lead all-woman expeditions and climbs.

I don't believe women are any more subject to fears than men. It is probably because they exhibit such a reverence for life and by nature are conservative as mothers that the impression of the "weaker sex" has persisted. A negative physical reaction to mice or snakes is not the bench mark of cowardice. Fear of the unknown is natural in any normal person. It is this normal fear that makes us all good students of techniques or disciplines that can eliminate the unknown. Caution and strict adherence to established safety standards are practical guidelines for the responsible expedition leader. And it is women's natural caution that makes them ideal candidates for leadership roles on extended expeditions, if they have learned the techniques and gained the experience required to grapple with all nature's forces—human nature as well as mother nature. Good leaders are not necessarily the biggest, strongest or oldest. Great climbing skill, woodsman- or woodswomanship, an elevated position in the business world, social prominence, or a college diploma does not necessarily mean a person will make the best outdoor expedition leader.

An expedition leader must be aware of all the elements of decision making. If one is going to influence and direct the behavior of others, he or she must begin by knowing all the basic rules for producing harmony and cooperation in tense situations. A pragmatic realist who makes no false claims, the outdoor woman should strive to be nonegotistical, free of sham or bluff, capable of good judgment under pressure, able to recognize talent and delegate jobs, talented at resisting aggressive challenges to her authority with grace and finality, receptive to the merit of conflicting opinions, articulate, sympathetic, sensitive, unselfish, aware, optimistic, witty enough to be able to diffuse a volatile situation, intelligent enough to anticipate problems, honest, humble, self-effacing if necessary, likeable and—most important—cool and steady.

You may not feel confident enough to act as leader unless it is over territory where you've had previous successful ventures. And you may want to designate someone else as joint leader and divide the chores of pre-planning. Being a joint leader requires congenial ongoing discussions about all plans before and during the trip.

To avoid the problems that arise when third parties overhear the issues under consideration and throw in their "two cents," you as leader or originator should lay down the ground rules in advance. If the group is small, the weather is mild, and the country is not dangerous, you might try the democratic process and give everyone a voice. This experience alone will make you realize the value of having a single authoritative leader on difficult expeditions.

Arlene Blum, leader of the AWHE climb of Annapurna in 1978, was asked before the attempt how she would handle leadership and decisions:

At high altitude, people don't get enough oxygen. It makes them moody and difficult. I will try to get a consensus, but there won't always be complete agreement. I want to be democratic, but I have the final say. They have all agreed to that.

I met and talked with Arlene about the climb before they departed, and I felt she could make that agreement stick. Good expedition behavior implies sticking to any pre-agreements. But at high altitude and under pressure, there is no enforcement mechanism available. The individual's reaction—acceptance or rejection—turns 50 percent on conditioned reflex and 50 percent on presentation, trust and respect.

What a Leader Does

Organizes and delegates responsibility

Schedules itineraries

Consults about permits or licenses

Interviews hikers, climbers and authorities

Excludes handicapped or unhealthy

Checks food, clothes, packs, equipment, etc.

Limits personal gear and weight

Arranges logistics

Collects for individual or group medical insurance

Obtains release of responsibility

Informs about rules of conduct, choosing tentmate, etc.

Designates photographer to supply pictures to group and press

Distributes maps and compasses

Carries first-aid and repair equipment

Sets mood and tone (light or serious)

As you know, until recently women had a hard enough time in the business world just making the team without thinking about being a leader or captain of industry. Through talent, motivation and realistic direction based on scientific investigation of the job market, career women have tripled their numbers in top management positions.

The same knowledge and techniques employed by the working woman apply also to securing a leadership role in the outdoor world of hiking and climbing. If other factors are equal, leadership in any area is based primarily on controlling relationships between people.

Margaret Henning and Anne Jardim have produced a controversial bestseller called *The Managerial Woman* from their own insights gained as corporate consultants and from studies of 3,000 women striving for a leadership role.

Interestingly, they found that men derived a significant advantage in the business world from playing team sports during their school years. Men said:

> "It was boys only
> Teamwork
> Hard work
> Preparation and practice, practice, practice
> If you were knocked down, you had to get up again
> It gave you a sense of belonging, of being part of something bigger than yourself
> You learned that a team needs a leader because motivation or lack of it depends on the coach
> You learned fast that some people were better than others—but you had to have 11 [players]"

What did you have to learn if you wanted to stay on the team?

"Competition—you had to win

Cooperation to get a job done—you had to work with guys you wouldn't choose as friends outside the team

If you got swell-headed about how fast you could run, then the other guys didn't block for you anymore

Losing—what it felt like to lose

That you win some and you lose some

How to take criticism—from the coach, your peers, the crowd

That you didn't get anywhere without planning, and you had to have alternative plans

Once you knew the rules, you could bend them— and you could influence the referee"

These are personal skills. Boys begin to develop them in an outdoor classroom to which girls traditionally have had no access. The prestigious sports for girls tend to be one-on-one: tennis, swimming, golf, gymnastics, skating. And in the one-on-one sports, the old adage that "it's not whether you won or lost but how you played the game" has been so stressed that many women tennis players now in their twenties still play for "exercise"—they don't play to win. While this is changing, it is changing slowly. There cannot be many fathers with the courage to face the ridicule that must have attached to the brave man who fought the sneering insistence of the Little League coach that his daughter wear a protective cup in order to qualify for the baseball team.

The nature of team sports—one team against another, each aiming to win, to each an objective— requires one to develop a strategy that takes the environment into account. Who and what can help?

Who and what can hinder? When? How much? How do I make use of this or counter that in order to get where I want to go? And if the objective is career advancement through the management ranks of today's corporation (or if the objective is leadership of a major mountain-climbing expedition), who is more likely to win—the man who sees the world as it is, a world of winning and losing, of teams, of stars, of average and mediocre players, or the woman who is struggling to find a world as it should be?

This does not mean that women should become more like men. It does mean that women as thinking people should assess much more concretely what is in it for them—what the costs and rewards of reaching their goal will be.

When a woman begins to feel the stirrings of desire to lead a major climbing expedition, I suggest that she first ask herself the following questions:

1. What would it take to stop waiting and start acting? To let people know what you want and what you're prepared to do to get it? To start asking questions about any major climbs in planning stages? To broaden contacts with climbers in other areas? To ask to learn new skills, to be given extra assignments, to take on new projects?

2. Are you suffering from internal conflicts that you have never consciously examined? The process of overcoming conflict involves bringing it out in the open, analyzing and evaluating it, coming to grips with it. Conflict not understood and not acted upon is a continual emotional drain.

3. If you're afraid to risk, why are you afraid? Do you see risk only in the negative? Do you think of risk

as an uncontrollable gamble rather than as an accessible and manageable act? Have you ever thought of risk-taking as something over which you might have a certain degree of control?

4. Have you tried to keep your career life and your personal life (sports) totally separate? You've probably tried fairly hard and thought it logical to do so. Think of the costs of this strategy. You may have to give up your strategy of separation, for it is both time-consuming and conflict-laden. As a man does, you may have to negotiate between roles, trading off time and energy in one today for time and energy in another next week. To begin, you will have to discuss the responsibilities you have at work and your desires for greater involvement in major climbs with your husband or anyone else who is involved in your personal life. If you haven't begun this process, it is critically important that you do so.

When you're ready to lead a major expedition of your own, you should first pick a mountain and interview experienced climbers and then get the recognition of the American Alpine Club. It is best to pick an interesting peak to attempt—one that has not been climbed much. A mountain in a foreign country, little exposed to the American press, is ideal. If possible, you should climb by an unclimbed route. I once tried to organize a joint American-Chinese co-ed team to climb a fabled peak on the Indian border, but that was before Nixon's trip and the Chinese Embassy in Canada would only respond politely. Nevertheless, the interest of the press and of gifted climbers in that proposal was spectacular.

The American Women's Himalayan Expedition of

1978 (often called the Annapurna climb by the press because of the famed first climb of Annapurna in 1950 by a French team and the publication of Maurice Herzog's book) began just that way. It was an idea—a dream—in the head of one person, Arlene Blum.

As you know, a Japanese woman had climbed Everest in 1975. Later that same year, Everest had been climbed by a Chinese woman. Polish women had climbed Gasherbrum 2 and 3. American women had played only a minor role in Himalayan climbing. Annapurna, the tenth highest mountain in the world (26,558 feet), had never been climbed by an American woman. In fact, no American woman had climbed any of the fourteen mountains in the world that are higher than 26,000 feet. Additional advantages of Annapurna were that it had not been climbed much even by men and that it did not require great use of oxygen, which is extremely expensive in remote areas.

Arlene Blum gathered together a few interested friends and they each got a few more, and it took off from there. The leaders let their plans be known to local climbing clubs, stores, etc., in Berkeley, California. After interviewing applicants, the leader Arlene climbed in the Sierra mountains with the likeliest candidates to determine capability. The first requirement was high altitude experience, of course.

When you have chosen your group, they should sign an agreement that all income from books, interviews, appearances, endorsements, etc., will go into one pot to pay for the expedition. As soon as the date of departure is established, a press release can be distributed to local news media. The expedition climbing group should be organized from the top, with duties and responsibilities for advance preparation to begin at once. Duties during the actual climb might be divided entirely differently.

To begin, you need people to handle finances, communications, photographs, supplies, travel, training, fund-raising, transportation, medicine, packing, shipping, etc. You'll want to take advantage of volunteers who will not make the climb but will give grass-roots support to your vision and assist with food packaging, logistics and fund-raising.

A Himalayan climb today is not the mind-boggling, awesome supply job it was before 1951. In Katmandu, Nepal, there is an Englishman named Mike Cheney, an ex-Gurka officer, who will arrange to hire Sherpas, provide certain supplies, and handle logistics of coordination with authorities, as he has done for many recent climbs through a company called "Sherpa Cooperative."

When the first contributions have provided the necessary bank balance, you as leader should make a reconnaissance trip to investigate routes and camps and to arrange for Sherpas. Everything has to arrive at the correct time, calculated for the best weather; medical assistance and replacement needs must be allowed for—all this is the leader's responsibility. For Annapurna and much of the rest of the Himalayas, the best weather is between summer monsoon and the cold winter winds. It is a short climbing season. Arlene and AWHE decided to use three high-altitude Sherpas and two female Sherpas to carry supplies and help establish camps. It was determined that base camp would be at 14,300 feet, and five more camps would be set up on the mountain. Several tons of food and equipment had to be transported to these camps before the summit could be attempted. Fortunately, the hard, tiring, tedious job of supplying these camps helps the climbers, porters and Sherpas acclimatize to increasingly high altitudes.

There have been some climbers above 26,500 feet without oxygen. But since oxygen does increase a climber's performance, warmth and mental abilities, it adds to safety. On Annapurna and other Himalayan climbs above 20,000 feet, oxygen and cylinders should be available for summit climbers, despite the weight and logistical problems.

The cost estimate for the AWHE climb was $80,000, broken down as follows:

Annapurna permit	$ 1,100
Food	8,000
Equipment	20,000
Radio	2,000
Oxygen and medical supplies	5,000
Shipping costs	10,000
Transportation	14,500
Customs duties	2,500
Salaries for porters	8,000
Salaries for Sherpas and liaison	1,900
Insurance for Sherpas and liaison	2,000
Contingency fund	5,000

You will get some idea of the reason for porters' salaries when you figure that from Katmandu in Nepal tons of gear had to be transported over 80 miles up rocky trails by backpack, a trip of ten days or more, during the summer monsoon of August. During September the base camp was established, and later five additional camps. Then the team began to prepare for an early October assault on the summit. The AWHE group decided to use a different route from that used by the French, who were caught in severe avalanches. The AWHE route is technically more difficult, for it involves scaling a buttress east of the original French route.

But just how does a women's group raise money?

First you print a brochure or extended booklet informing the public about the climb, its purpose, etc., and asking for contributions. If you are recognized by the American Alpine Club, they may receive funds for you, as they did for the AWHE.

The AWHE brochure featured pictures of climbers and of the mountain and a route map. The text included objectives, history, dates, cost, camps, logistics, explanations, etc., all of which the leaders had discussed long before departure. It was circulated to many clubs, businesses, organizations, manufacturers, retail sporting goods stores and interested individuals. Potential sponsors were advised that "each dollar you contribute will get a climber five feet closer to the summit" and "anyone contributing $15 or more will receive a postcard showing Annapurna, carried by runners from base camp and signed by all the women on the trip."

The AWHE group even thought of having an expedition sponsors' trek to Nepal to help support their expedition—in a sense a traveling fan club. The plan called for one group of beginners and one of climbers to arrive at Annapurna base camp about the time the advanced climbers were making their attempt on the summit.

Then you might consider selling posters, postcards

and T-shirts. The AWHE had sold over 8,000 shirts at $8 and $10 by the end of August 1978. Shirts said "A Woman's Place Is on Top" over a drawing of the mountain. A line below said "American Women's Himalayan Expeditions." Retail sporting goods stores and other outlets handled sales without taking a percentage—they thus contributed by acting as a collection agency.

Next, you sell magazine, book and film rights if you can. The AWHE signed with *National Geographic* for a figure that might go as high as $16,000 and with Crowell for a $30,000 advance on a book.

If the T-shirts make $8,000 or $10,000 total, that's $54,000, plus the private contributions of individuals to make up the $26,000 difference.

The AWHE group tapped a rich vein of identity and sympathy in the American public. Women interested in organizing similar climbs on their own should take note that the appeal was based on the failure of American women climbers to match the accomplishments of women of other nations. The brochure stated:

> *High altitude expeditionary mountaineering requires many skills which can only be developed through experience. There are very few women in this country who have had the opportunity to participate in expeditions to major peaks. Through organizing their own expedition, ten American women will have the opportunity to increase their high altitude mountaineering skills.*
>
> *[They] will venture into another level of reality–into the rarefied world of high altitude expedition climbing. What is to be gained? The stakes are high and so is the reward: affirmation for all women–the shared vision of ourselves as courageous and capable, and, as with all great visions, the appeal is universal.*

And here is a letter the American Women's Himalayan Expedition received from a male supporter:

> *I assume that some or all of these women belong to the women's liberation movement. This money ($20) comes to you from an anti-women's libber who nevertheless admires their courage and wishes them luck in the success in the venture. Please accept. . . . I work as a press operator in a small factory and do not have a lot of money, but if you fall short of your money goal, just prior to your scheduled departure, write to me and maybe I will be able to donate a little more ($50). Any more than that (up to $2,000) would have to be on trust, an interest-free loan. That's how much for some reason that expedition of yours means to me.*

Looking forward to long-range achievements, the 1978 members have set up a permanent organization, the American Women's Himalayan Expeditions, which they hope will fund future climbs in the Himalayan area. Presumably, any money left over from the Annapurna climb will go to the permanent organization.

15 | BASIC CLIMBING

Rocks make no compromise for sex. . . . Rock climbing is not like some sports, where it is made easier for women; or sports like, say, softball, which is only baseball for soft people. On a rock, everything is equal.

—Beverly Johnson

It has been said that women are often more natural climbers than men because they must rely on technique rather than brute strength. Sam Moses, in *Sports Illustrated,* said, "They have better bodies for climbing than men. The ideal body for a rock climber would be that of a fourteen-year-old girl about five feet eight inches tall with shoulders of a channel swimmer and legs of a hurdler. Female suppleness is their greatest asset. The contortions of a climber's positions often produce dislocations and other injuries."

But it is in the head where all the solutions are found before a move is made; thus a woman must develop a mechanical and technical mind, even though her interests may not have leaned in that direction in the past. The problems encountered in rock climbing can be likened to those of chess. A climber can be momentarily stalled at any point on the face of a cliff, searching the rocks around her for toeholds and handholds, trying to figure the next move. She may make several that do not work before she finds one that does. And, as in chess, a climber must plan her moves ahead to avoid climbing herself into a checkmate.

Considering the penalty, checkmating yourself on a cliff is hardly like being checkmated by an opponent on a chessboard. On either board or cliff, it is inevitable that a player will be checked; it is in the price you pay that the comparison ends. Chess is a labor of the mind. Rock climbing is total physical and mental labor. However, both are a personal challenge in which the creative solutions are endless.

The pieces in the climbing game are fewer than in chess, but they have relative values. The rope is your King. With it you can move up or down the cliff in straight lines. *Pitons* and *chocks* begin as pawns. *Pitons* are large steel spikes, each with a hole to attach a rope or carabiner, that are driven into cracks with a hammer; *chocks* are rectangular aluminum blocks in different sizes, with steel cable loops attached, that are wedged into cracks without the use of hammers, to anchor and belay like pitons. They give you safety in numbers, and you Queen them by removing them as you go for multiple use on the same cliff. Adding to the arsenal of pieces that broaden your moves and checkmate escapes are *stirrups, pulleys,* and *carabiners,* which are like giant oblong safety pins for attaching to pitons (only when you depress the springgate will they open in an inward direction to accept a rope); *Swami belts,* also called *diaper slings,* which are waist and buttocks harnesses worn by climbers to attach themselves by carabiners to a rope that will sometimes be anchored to pitons or chocks in cracks on the side of a cliff; and *shoulder slings,* which are short loops of rope that fit over one shoulder and are for carrying étrier hardware attached to carabiners for ready use.

These bits of hardware are all pieces or tools used in aid-climbing as opposed to free-climbing. Aid-climbing techniques can be highly complex. Entire books have been written on this subject alone (see Bibliography).

Free-climbing, which involves only the use of a rope, is where we all begin. Free-climbing of even short routes for an afternoon or a couple of hours can be one of life's greatest escapes. The use of head and body without competition in fresh air can be as therapeutic as transcendental meditation.

The Rope

Most climbing hardware is indestructible, but a climbing rope is fragile and expensive. It should be studied and cared for. Some climbers will use only their own rope and have a loving relationship with it, like a combat marine with his "fieldpiece." Paul Petzoldt suggests that the rope be given the same respect one would give a lethal weapon, which makes the point in just two words. As with boots, I recommend the best—twisted nylon manufactured especially for climbing. It can cost $70 to $150 for a standard United States length of 120 or 150 feet in a choice of diameters: ⅜ inch or $7/16$ inch. A woman or a party of women climbing are very safe on a ⅜-inch rope which is tested to hold 3,000 pounds. One $7/16$ inch in diameter which tests to 4,000 pounds is usually used for teaching because of the considerable wear and the increased probability of long falls.

A nylon rope can be damaged by heat or by contact with oil or gasoline. It can be rinsed on occasion to clean dirt and tiny flakes of rock; however, you must dry it in the shade.

Rope will untwist unless the ends are fused in the following manner. Tape the last two inches; then place the end on a board and, with razor or knife, cut off one inch in a straight, perfect cut. Hold the end over a two-inch flame from a cigarette lighter or several wooden matches until the fiber ends fuse together. Be very careful you do not allow other sides of the rope to burn or drip hot nylon on the sides of the rope. After cooling, remove the tape and dip one inch of the rope end into a hard epoxy glue. The ends of your rope should be marked with different colors for identification, either with tape or paint. If you are using two ropes, the second rope's end colors should not match the first rope's. The middle of a rope should also be marked.

Your first rope skill should be coiling and uncoiling. You can't even handle or move an uncoiled rope from place to place without its becoming an endless snake.

To coil, sit to the right side of a pile of rope. Grasp the rope a foot from the end with your right hand (left-handed people can substitute "left" for "right"), and rest that hand palm up on your right knee. Run your left hand out along the long end of the rope to arm's length. Bring the rope around your knees and up across your right palm. (You can run it around your toes instead of your knees if it is easier for you.) If there are kinks in the rope, hold it steady with your right hand while you snap them out with your left. Repeat until there remain only 5 or 6 feet of rope.

Now lift the coil up and bend it so you can hold it

between your knees. Make a loop with 15 inches of the remaining rope and place the loop on top of coil. With the rest of the rope, make a half hitch around the coil at the open end of the loop; continue to wrap the rest of the rope around the coil, and finish by pulling the remaining foot of rope through the loop and tightening.

A twisted rope should be restacked to free kinks. Hold the rope with one hand and pull it through the palm of your other hand. When kinks appear, whip them out in the natural direction to free twists.

The wrong knot can be as lethal a weapon as the wrong rope. A square knot can come undone if it catches on points of rocks or stumps—its use in inappropriate situations has resulted in many climbing accidents.

The half hitch is simply a loop used to wrap one rope under another. Several half hitches can be used in sequence to secure the loose ends after another knot has been tied.

The bowline is used to tie oneself to the end of a rope. With the rope running behind your back, hold an end with a 15-inch tail in your right hand in front of your body at waist height. The rope should come between your thumb and your forefinger, knuckles up. Hold the longer end of rope in your left hand, and form a loop in it at belt height. The end of the rope emerging from around your body should be on top of the longer main end. Pass the rope in your right hand through that main loop from below. Loop it under and around the long end of the rope, and bring it back down through the loop so that it runs back parallel to itself. Take up the slack and tighten; then do a couple of half hitches with the remaining

Coiling and tying rope.

Completing the bowline.

tail. This is the same knot used when tying a rope to one's harness.

The double bowline simply involves making two loops in the main rope before tying with the short end. The second loop should be beneath the first loop. For use over an extended period of time, it is recommended above all other knots. Whenever a rope is available, you would do well to practice coiling and knotting in order to adapt to various textures, weights and stiffnesses.

Each time a rope is used, it should be inspected. If someone falls with a rope, it should again be inspected before reuse. It can easily get stretched or worn from use over rough edges. If one or more strands are broken, it should not be used for climbing.

Dress

A woman rock climber will have to make one concession that her feminine nature may resent—she will have to accept the fact that using her hands in a physical way will toughen and scar them. It is not generally possible to use gloves for climbing. Tight-fitting leather gloves can be used for some rope work to prevent burns, but bare hands are necessary for free-climbing of even the simplest nature. Nivea hand cream and petroleum jelly can be used afterwards to lubricate dry skin and scars, but not while you are climbing.

Long hair is also a serious hazard. It can get caught in a rope or harness, or obstruct eyesight. Hair should be tied back securely under a bandanna to keep it clean and controlled. This makes the head size compact

Opposite: Friction climbing.

in case the need to wear a helmet arises at some point. Some women climbers with pierced ears prefer wearing small or button-type earrings. Loop earrings should be avoided, for they are apt to catch on branches.

Depending on the weather, dress in either loose-fitting pants or knickers. Leather shorts are the favorite summer wear of the Swiss because they are thick and padded against the rope. A wool sweater or shirt, tight-fitting climbing shoes with Vibram soles, and two ropes will complete your day-climbing outfit.

Technique

Again, it is the feet that are the foundation for most climbing—a foot in a stiff-soled shoe can hold you on a narrow ledge. The hands are used mainly for balance and to hold you against the wall. Most beginning climbers make the mistake of keeping their hands and body as close to the wall as possible, thus creating an outward leverage on their feet that could spring them loose. The body should be kept as nearly perpendicular to the horizon as possible so that there is a balance with gravity at toe level at all times. Handholds are used only for security. The climber with her knees bent and her buttocks away from the wall is creating a pinch force like that of a spring clip; the friction where hands and feet contact rock is delicate but quite sufficient for relaxed purchase—the very opposite of the "rock hugging" which the fearful beginner is usually prone to attempt.

There is a certain personal rhythm one develops for each climb that combines breathing with the larger movements. It is based on keeping three contact points in touch with the mountain at all times for maximum friction, moving only one support limb to a new position at any one time, and shifting body weight to a new direction only after making a new grip. In this manner, the climber always divides her total body weight between these points at once and therefore puts the least possible amount of strain on any one hold, whether feet or hands. With experience, the climber develops a subconscious feel of rhythmic needs and a breathing pace to fit her body strength which will cause her to appear to flow up the cliff in a smooth motion rather than in fits and starts. The catlike ability of a natural climber to shift weight distribution is almost impossible to analyze.

A foothold will seldom be big enough for the entire boot. That is why a tight-fitting boot with a stiff-edged sole is best for rock climbing. You do not want your foot to shift inside your boot if you have only ¼ inch of rock holding your 130 pounds. Use your big toe on small outcroppings. In large vertical cracks turn your foot sideways; use a contact of toe and heel if the crack fits your foot. If you are in a wide chimney, position one boot sole flat against the wall crack on the left side and grip the right wall with the full sole of the other foot. On narrow ledges, use of the inside sole gives the best foot contact, but it tends to draw the body tight to the wall, which might act as a fulcrum, springing legs and feet off the ledge.

The main muscles of the legs should be used to gain height. Avoid reaching handholds way above your head; try to grasp at or below shoulder height. "Pull" handholds from above the shoulders use more energy and strength, and place extra strain on fingers and hands. Pushing up with hands and feet is preferred to pulling or muscling up.

Hands can be used in all manner and form to hold

onto the mountain. Jamming the fist into narrow cracks; pulling on a crack with both hands facing outward as though you were trying to force open a door; even pushing with your palm up against the bottom of a rock ledge—all can give security if your feet are well placed. There is the squeezing-from-outstretched-arms position and even simple finger- or thumbholds.

The layback is a special technique for climbing near-vertical cracks. You pull against the upper side of the crack with your hands while "walking" up the lower edge.

In friction climbing, however, you are not dependent on cracks or toeholds. It is the friction of your hands and feet, combined with the force of gravity, that holds you on the mountain.

Experienced climbers are confident they will not fall—unless they overstep their ability or get careless. To them, a fall is misjudgment or loss of control or maybe recklessness, which would be the absolute worst. A climbing fool is scorned. The risks a rock climber takes are those she chooses. Climbers don't believe their sport is dangerous, because they control the risk—most like making difficult moves away from their protection not for the thrill of danger, but to experience the feeling of control through confidence.

Rock climbers will tell you they gamble on no one's mercy. The expedition mountain climber is at the mercy of the weather; the auto racer is at the mercy of mechanical things; and a hang glider pilot tosses his fate to the wind—"but a rock climber calls all the shots."

That was probably truer in the age of pitons, when it was often said, "He carries his courage in a

Above: Handjam.   *Below left:* Fistjam.   *Right:* Toehold.

rucksack." In the last ten years, climbers in general have come to scorn the use of pitons on aesthetic and ecological grounds. Pitons are sometimes left behind in the wall, and they reduce the challenge of finding a route. The sight of these metal spikes pounded in with a hammer during an earlier climb spoils the challenge of deciding which route to take. Old pitons are spoilsports, rudely reminding a climber that someone has been there before. However, all the big walls take more than a day to climb and require aids, so climbers must be experienced with aids if they want to do the ultimate climb.

THE BELAY

The belay is the basic rope technique used to prevent a fall. It must be learned before all other techniques, and your instruction should include experiencing a practice fall.

To practice, stretch out your rope as though a climber were tied to the other end. Then sit facing the climber with the rope on your left. Bring the rope behind your back below the waist, and hold the end with your right hand. Your left hand should be stretched out in front, holding the rope leading to the climber on the end. If the climber falls, you, the belayer, can catch him by holding fast with your right hand and the rope friction around your body. Use your right hand to secure the rope keeping your arm bent and your hand pressed near your waist in order to keep your weight on your hips. This is the first stage of three.

Now, with your left hand, pull the rope up; simultaneously push forward with your right hand so that

Opposite: Layback.

the rope slides freely around your hips. The left hand thus pulls up one arm's length of rope and the right pushes a length. The left hand is now holding the rope near your waist, and the right arm is extended along the rope toward the climber. The right hand grips the rope at all times to prevent a fall. This is the second stage.

Now slide your left hand forward without releasing, so that it is ahead of your right hand. Then quickly grip both ropes with the fingers of your left hand while sliding your right hand back to beginning position at your waist. This grip allows the left hand to release one rope while still maintaining a hold on the climber's rope. The left arm remains extended. The retrieved extra rope is dropped at your side. You have now completed the third stage of the shifting belay.

If the belayer is left-handed, she may need to do belay in reverse, so that she can secure the belay with her strongest hand.

There are many possible belay positions. The safest is to sit down and brace your feet against a rock with your knees stiff. The rope to the climber should run between your legs—which should be spread apart so weight will not tip you.

The voice signals used in actual climbs are a critical communications shorthand that you should rehearse with each new climbing partner before the two of you do any climbing together. It is best to actually extend ropes between you in full dress rehearsal—each exchanging positions to shout signals. On real climbs you often cannot see each other, and protruding rocks or high wind can make hearing difficult.

On Belay	Tells climber that her belayer is in position and ready.
Climbing	Tells belayer that climber heard her and is ready to climb.
Climb	Tells climber that belayer expects her to climb now.
Belay off	Tells belayer that climber has reached security and she can release belay.
Thank you	Tells climber that belayer has heard and will relax.
Up rope	Tells belayer to take up slack. She responds with "thank you," so that climber will know she heard.
Slack	Tells belayer that climber needs a slow pendant. Belayer says "thank you."
Tension	Tells belayer to take up slack fast. She answers "thank you."
Climbing with tension	Tells belayer to pull as hard as she can with left hand, holding belay with right hand. Belayer answers "climb."
Slack with tension	Tells belayer the reverse of "climbing with tension"; i.e., to give tight rope.

Falling	Tells belayer to brace her position and grip, because climber senses that she is slipping. Belayer tenses legs and brings right hand with rope around her body to the left. This ensures adequate friction against body to prevent rope from slipping.

RAPPELLING

Probably the most commonly used rope maneuver is the rappel. The fastest method of descending over a dangerous or steep section, it involves sliding down a rope.

First, calculate the length of rope needed to reach the bottom, and double that amount. For example, if a rope is 150 feet, it can be used for a rappel of 75 feet. If the distance to be descended is greater than 75 feet, two ropes, joined, are necessary. (Also, a second rope is handy for belaying an injured or inexperienced person on rappel.) The double rope length is needed not for safety but to allow the rope to circle (as opposed to having one end tied to) objects such as a rock or tree, so that the rope can then be retrieved by pulling a single end from the bottom. The rate of descent is controlled by the rope's friction around the climber's body. You will use a separate rope, tied to you, as a safety.

To practice rappelling, loop the center of your rope around a tree, or use a sling around a rock, and then flip both ends of the rope down the cliff. (A sling is substituted to prevent wear on a rope during practice.) Straddle the rope, facing the anchor.

With the rope between your legs, reach behind you with your left hand and lift both ropes. Bring them around your left leg and up over your left shoulder. The rope passes from behind your left buttocks under your left armpit to the front of your chest, then diagonally down across your back and under your right armpit, where it is grasped by the right hand. The right arm is extended forward from waist level, with your palm up, holding rope. With your knees stiffened and your feet apart, push backward until you feel a tightening of the rope through your crotch and on your back.

The right hand is used to control the rate of descent. Rope friction around the climber's body takes the strain off the hand. As long as the rope is in body contact, friction against the back and the tightening of the right hand will act as a brake. This method of rappel is called the Swiss Body Rappel. Climbers practicing this technique should wear protective clothing to avoid rope burns. Caution should be taken, especially by women, to slide the rope over the left buttock, not directly into the crotch. A quicker and easier rappel method, and one with less friction, is to allow the rope between the legs to come up over the left shoulder from behind and then across the front, where the right hand holds it and acts as a brake. This method is practical for short nonvertical pitches.

To begin, one must choose the rappelling site with care. Natural anchorage must be stable. If not, chocks or pitons will have to be used. Drive one into each of two separate cracks located close together. Attach carabiners to each piton, and run the rope through both, so that if one pulls out, the other will act as a safety measure. The use of pitons or blocks as aids should be avoided, however, until you feel confident at free-climbing.

The safest procedure when rappelling is to use two carabiners side by side to hold the sling and the ropes. Snap carabiners onto the sling with gates down and facing you. To snap in the rappel rope, twist the carabiners until the gates face outside and up. You should make it a habit to always attach double carabiners with gates facing opposite each other before you begin descent. You could also use a figure 8 descender, as shown in the photograph.

Proper position for rappelling is with your feet about a foot apart, your body leaning forward from the hips, your legs straight. Feet should be kept low against rocks to carry a part of your weight as you back down the cliff, and your right arm should be kept straight except when you want to apply more friction by swinging it to the front. Care must be taken before and during the descent to inspect the route for loose rocks that might later be dislodged by rope action and fall on you. It might be advisable to knock rocks loose or choose a new route.

When you reach the bottom, remove the rappel rope, untie the safety rope, and step out of range of falling rocks, if possible. You should shout "off rappel" and advise the next climber to come down with caution.

The last climber to rappel should check rope settings to make sure they can be retrieved from the bottom. If pitons were used, the carabiners should be removed and an expendable sling between both pitons substituted, since pitons cannot be removed.

It is advisable to practice not only rappelling, but

Above: **Belay.**

Below: **Rappelling.**

Figure 8 descender.

Carabiner brake bar attached to harness with double carabiner.

rope retrieval methods as well. Imagine this perfect checkmating by two climbers: The scene is a simple two-stage rappel down a rock cliff in late afternoon. The climbers will descend to a ledge, then rappel on down the ledge to reach camp by nightfall. This means tying a sling around the lip of the rock cliff and retrieving the rappel rope to make a second descent. When both climbers have reached the ledge, they realize they forgot to untie the knot in one end of the rappel rope. They see this only after the rope is 20 feet above their heads. It might go through the sling, but they don't know that for sure. They attempt to free-climb up to untie the knot, but there are no handholds available. They then try to pull the knot through the sling. After an hour of jiggling the rope in all manner of arcs, they realize that they can't loosen the rope; but they can't climb up the rope to untie the knot because they're not sure it's safe. (The knot is not tied into the sling—it is just caught by the pressure of weight against the ledge.) They have checkmated themselves. The sun is setting. What do they do? They use belay rope to do a second rappel, and they repeat the entire climb the next day to recover the first rope. If they don't have a belay rope, they stay on the ledge overnight; it may be days before someone rescues them. That's the penalty of checkmate.

An account of a memorable climb in Yosemite, from my 1971 diary:

Instead of the good fingercracks we'd hoped for, a few hard face moves had led me to a shallow groove, nearly vertical for one five-foot section and only big enough for fingertips. The smooth granite on either side was frustratingly hold-less. . . . I was totally checked.

Even standing in a sling, I could not find any holds that seemed usable to pass the section free. I was pretty disappointed and just stared down at trees and lichen at eye level, not really considering the fact that my partner might do better.

As soon as she could undo her anchor, Baba took off up the pitch. Since she was in shorts, she had gotten quite cold belaying, and it was only a minute or so before she reached the stance below the summit crack. Even here she didn't pause very long. Not long enough to realize how hard it was, because, either shivering with cold or charged with adrenaline, she free-climbed right up past the impossible part I had aided. I craned my neck to see over the edge, shouting down advice and encouragement. Unfortunately, I had placed a nut in a crucial fingerjam, and Baba couldn't quite hang on long enough to figure out an alternative move. She grabbed the sling to reach the stance. I was happy, though. . . . On her fifth try, she made it, discovering a vital foot sequence on what she later claimed was to be her final attempt. I couldn't see her, but I felt the rope feed out past the point where I knew she'd passed the move. A nearly hysterical yell for slack assured me she was now finishing off the final fingerjamming onto the stance. She was too excited to rest long and quickly finished the last few feet to the top.

I could tell she was pleased with herself. On many, even most of the hard climbs we attempted together, Baba would adopt an almost indifferent attitude toward the whole project. Once up, she would seem to consider the ascent merely a job completed. Today was different. She tried to keep it to herself, but soon gave up; she was bubbling with content. . . .

Distracted, I followed the pitch on my next attempt and smiled with gratitude for whatever got me up. Despite positive preaching to my subconscious, I'd felt in the seat of my pants I would not be able to do it, reasonable explanation unknown, I just did. . . .

Without a doubt that move had turned out to be one of the most difficult either of us had ever done, and it was very

rewarding to be the creators of it. It was fingery and desper-
ately thin and brought beads of sweat and adrenaline jitters
just thinking about it. It would be nearly a week before I
grew tired of discussing its idiosyncrasies and reminding
Baba just how hard it was. We bushwhacked down off the
cliff, stopped briefly to gather our gear at the base, then
strode out to the car.

Climbing Grades and Classifications

To appreciate the art of and to engage safely in the
challenge of climbing, it is vital that you have some
understanding of the "mountaineering fraternities"
(an expression that also was meant to include
sororities), efforts to grade and classify the degrees of
difficulty one will encounter in attempting to scale a
particular route. The first efforts to organize a standard of communication began in the Alps when
climbers decided to develop a history and guidebook
for future generations.

All classification systems have the same objective: to
analyze and evaluate the routes by compact, accepted
recognized rating symbols. They are all imperfect.
But the conscience and frustration of later climbers
has helped to improve each description as the climbing traffic on a route increases. On seldom-traveled
routes, the ratings reflect the skill or ego of only a few
climbers, or often weather conditions during the
climb. And since you don't know the author, you cannot accurately compare your abilities. At best any
climbing classification is an approximation. I thought
it best to give a full explanation of the UIAA method,
adopted from the publication "UIAA Climbing and
Classification System." By using the comparative chart
on page 230 one can then interpret the American

Decimal System, which sometimes is referred to as the Sierra Club System.

The efforts of the systems' designers to save time and space with shorthand ratings and climbing directions are virtually defeated by the amount of explanation and study required to learn the overlapping systems. Many good climbers I've spoken to have great difficulty making a perfect interpretation, but even imperfect information is an invaluable asset when one is attempting a new route. In other words, the alternative—having no advance advice before an attempt—is really no alternative at all. This section should be re-read and studied after you have had some experience in the mountains and with the use of a terrain map.

UIAA CLIMBING AND CLASSIFICATION SYSTEM

Descriptions of climbs make a clear distinction between the evaluation of "free" climbing and that of climbing using artificial aids. Thus, if a route or parts of it is graded as "free," it must be understood that pitons, edges, slings, nuts or other aids are used only for protection and not for progression. The grading for climbing that is entirely "free" is expressed by the Roman numerals I to VI. The addition of a + (plus) and a − (minus) to grades III through VI makes available fourteen separate grades. The ultimate achievements in rock climbing lie in "free" and not in "artificial" climbing.

Following is an explanation of the six main grades:

Grade I.   Least difficult kind of climbing on rock— but not just on walking terrain. The hands are being used on the rock for balance. Beginners should be secured and roped.

Grade II. Moderate difficulties involved. Correct use of hand- and footholds important. Experienced climbers usually go without the use of the rope (or go together on long Alpine-type climbs between the difficult pitches on a short rope, carrying part of it coiled up). If belaying, this should be done with self-belay.

Grade III. Somewhat greater difficulties involved. Upper limit for occasional climbers. May demand some output of strength. Knowledge of good belay technique, correct self-belaying, and rappelling is necessary. Some pitons, nuts, carabiners, slings and a hammer should be carried just to be prepared for the unexpected.

Grade IV. Great difficulties involved. Only for the experienced climber with regular training. Good technique and secure self-belays are necessary. Longer pitches are generally protected by pitons, nuts, slings, etc.

Grade V. Very great difficulties involved. Only for very good climbers with great endurance and experience. Belays between stands through pitons—with double rope—are absolutely necessary. Great output of strength and refined technique demanded.

Grade VI. Extraordinary difficulties involved. Only for the absolute top echelon. Tiniest handholds demand extraordinary finger strength (special training necessary). Superior balance and flexibility, great overall strength, courage, and good nerves required. Greatest exposure, with the stands often very tiny and tiresome. Free pitches are often combined with aid pitches. Much material to be carried. Even for the extraordinary climber in best training, the surmounting of a route designated VI+

(decimal grading 5.10 to 5.11) represents climbing on the border of falling and is at the limit of the humanly possible. Under winter conditions, such climbs are possible only with the extensive use of aids.

The artificial grades are explained as follows: A0 indicates that pitons and other aids are placed relatively easily and that the passages demand relatively low output of strength, endurance and courage. Stirrups are normally considered necessary. A2 through at least A4 indicate ever-increasing difficulties in placing aids and climbing over them.

THE AMERICAN DECIMAL SYSTEM

In the American Decimal System there are six classes: 1, 2, 3, 4, 5 and A (for aid). Class 5 (free roped climbing) has been subdivided into twelve classes labeled 5.0 to 5.11 to exactly define the difficulty of free-climbing. Class A has also been subdivided from 1 to 5 (A1, A2, etc.). (These classes are the same as the artificial UIAA grades.) In this rating system the score given to a climb is based on the most difficult move. If only one pitch on a climb reaches the 5.8 level, the entire climb is classed 5.8. If the climb has an aid move, it is rated with the highest number assigned to any aid move on the climb—for example, 5.8-A3.

Class 1 *A hike.* No hands needed.
Class 2 *A scramble.* Hands needed; rope not needed.
Class 3 *Easy climbing.* A scramble with hands, with use of simple technique. Rope available if needed.
Class 4 *Roped climbing* with belay. Belay anchored using hardware or natural anchors. This

would be Class 5 except that the pitches are short and there is lots of natural protection—trees, bushes, horns.

Class 5 *Roped climbing.* Protection, pitons, chocks, runners, etc., needed in addition to belay.

Class A *Roped climbing* with artificial assists—pre-tied stirrups, slings in sequence (foot or piton).

In addition to a class, each climb also has a grade. Class refers to and rates only the technical climbing difficulties. Following are the grades.

Grade I The class or technical section can be accomplished in a few hours.

Grade II The class or technical section can be accomplished in a half a day.

Grade III The class or technical section can be accomplished in most of a day.

Grade IV The class or technical section can be accomplished in a long day. (Class 5.7 would be the minimum for hardest pitch.)

Grade V The class or technical section can be accomplished in one and a half to two and a half days. (Class 5.8 would be the minimum for hardest pitch.)

Grade VI The class or technical section can be accomplished in two or more days with lots of difficult free- and aid-climbing.

A Class 5.7 climb in low country next to the road might be a Grade 2, but a climb with moves of the same class of technical difficulty high on a peak, if they occurred frequently during many rope leads of Classes 4 and 5, could be a Grade IV or Grade V climb.

Climbers should guard against assuming that accomplishing a certain grade climb automatically guarantees success for all climbs of that same grade. Grade is a rough measure that can only approximate an evaluation. Remember, grades have been compiled by different people in different time periods all over the world. Each climber must assume responsibility for analyzing all factors of each climb against his or her own known ability. As long as you keep in mind that classifications of climbs are subject to error, you should find them useful in choosing routes within your demonstrated abilities.

The UIAA System Compared to the American Decimal System

UIAA	Decimal	Explanations
I	1	Easy
II	2 and 3	
III −	4	Moderate
III	5	
III +	5.1	Moderately difficult
IV −	5.2	
IV	5.3	Difficult
IV +	5.4	
V −	5.5	
V	5.6	Very difficult
V +	5.7 to 5.8	
VI −	5.8 to 5.9	
VI	5.9 to 5.10	Extremely difficult
VI +	5.10 to 5.11	

Guidebook Descriptions

The description-head for a route ideally contains the following information:

1. Names and dates of first ascent.
2. Degree of the hardest pitch. If most of the pitches are of a lower standard, this will be indicated. If a route has both free and artificial pitches, they will be separately assessed according to their respective norms.
3. Total number of the "Standard Pitons" in the route.
4. Attributes of the route, such as exposed or poorly protected, physically demanding, often or mostly overhanging; information on objective dangers, such as falling stones or ice, rotten rock, waterfalls, pitches with water ice, difficult or complicated route-finding, necessity of friction or crack climbing, prevalence of bad weather or storms, difficult or close to impossible nature of return from above a point.
5. Total length and height of the route, with length of the key pitches and places for bivouacs.
6. Material (pitons, slings, etc.) recommended to take on the climb and recommended length of rope.
7. Average times for ascent and descent.
8. Best time of year.
9. Comments on overall quality of route. Comparison, particularly for long and difficult routes, with a popular climb of similar standard in the same area and also with an internationally known climb in another mountain range.
10. Location of and approaches to the route.
11. After the description-head comes the detailed description, in which, particularly for the longer routes, the degrees for the main pitches must be

given. For pitches which are mostly surmounted by using a piton for hand- or footholds the artificial A0 grade will be given, followed (where known) by the considerably more difficult free Roman grade number.

The technical difficulties of snow and ice climbs cannot be described with the usual grades, since they depend on conditions at the time, and no standard has been established for this. (For instance, an ice wall with a cover of frozen snow can be straightforward climbing, but if it is bare ice it can present a most strenuous and difficult problem.) In the description of such routes, the inclination of the ice and snow slopes and ice walls will be given as precisely as possible. Any danger of avalanches, cornices, etc., should be pointed out. If the route is a combination of ice and rock, the rock pitches will be graded in the normal way. With the further development of mountaineering at the very highest altitudes, some additions to this system will become necessary in the future.

In addition to the description of the route of ascent, there will be a precise description of the easiest route of descent from the summit to the base of the climb; directions to turn left or right are always given as if the climber were facing the valley. The places for rappelling and the location of rings fixed for rappelling may also be mentioned.

Following is an example of a guidebook description from *The Wind River Range* by Orrin H. Bonney and Lorraine G. Bonney:

Petzoldt's Pinnacle Ridge
   ... *An invigorating ridge with short rock scrambles and many spires. Excellent for amateurs with a good leader. Rope*

necessary; a traverse (combination Rtes. 1 & 3) is an all-day climb unless all difficulties are bypassed. Some difficulty locating highest point, a large balanced block of rock with summit records & cairn.

Rte. 1. N. Ridge. *II. 5.2. From Glacier Pass (152/2) traverse ridge S. turning 2–3 difficult towers to W. The last tower before the little notch where Rte. 2 reaches the ridge overhangs the notch—avoid by a delicate traverse on W. face at notch level, thus attaining notch and returning to ridge. Follow ridge to summit. This is only obligatory deviation from true ridge.*

Route-finding

Route-finding is a craft of experience and judgment. Experience here does not refer to having made Class 5.10 climbs on granite or Himalayan peaks, but to having climbed under various seasonal conditions on all kinds of surfaces, with aid and otherwise, as well as having interpreted guidebooks of varying age from different locales. It takes time to develop an eye for the weak spots on a mountain that will let a climber "go"; *that* becomes judgment.

Guidebook standards vary from one area to another. A description may sometimes give the impression that a route is an easy pitch, when in fact there are serious difficulties and real exposure, although the continual improvements in equipment design make the opposite situation more common. Interpreting artificial chock use on a route that was being climbed with pitons when the guidebook was written is another matter.

Judgment would also dictate allowing a margin for one's ability. One may be skilled in climbing on granite with cracks that give security for finger and toe jams, but feel nervous, exposed and frigid when

friction-climbing for the first time on an angled slab.
A veteran of granite would likewise find fragmented
sedimentary rock hairy the first time. And all have
good and bad days; our mood and other variables can
be hard to measure. The fact that you made a difficult
climb on a good day with super effort on a personal
high certainly doesn't mean that all future climbs of
the same grade are within your reach. Monica
Jackson says, "Innocence is knowing you can; experience is knowing you can't."

Route-finding is one of the most intriguing aspects
of climbing. Puzzling out the route is the game that
intrigues and challenges a person's imagination and
logic. We then see if our skill and body can make our
conclusions work out right. I know climbers who read
the guidebooks but then leave them home. They prefer to study the mountain from a distance, then find
their own route. They abhor following in someone
else's foot and hand path. It is through the need for
route-finding that one fulfills a love affair with a certain mountain. I was fascinated to learn in Whymper's
book how he puzzled out the logical solution to the
first summit climb of the Matterhorn in 1865. All attempts by him and others to reach the top from the
Italian side had failed because the mountain's slabs all
stopped toward Rome. With the eye of an artist, he
had drawn much mountain scenery; he could see
even without the aid of a plane or reconnaissance—
just from getting distance at an angle—that the other
side of the Matterhorn would form angled steps perfect for his purpose. The lay of the strata in sedimentary structure is a basic point in analyzing a route for a
climb:

*If the strata is tilted downward into the peak the resulting
upslab is so much the better; holds are abundant and even*

loose rocks tend to hold firmly in place. On downslab not only are the holds upside down from the climber's viewpoint but loose rocks tend to slide. . . .

A climber searching out a route on snow and ice is like a sailor trying to navigate on a surfboard. However, as Whymper writes,

. . . the inviting aspect of a couloir in morning, contrasted with the forbidding menace of its enclosing cliffs, frequently proves in afternoon to have been a crocodile smile. Gullies are the garbage chutes of mountains, and however quiet they may be during night begin with the sun to transport toward sea level such rubbish as avalanching snow, rocks loosened by frost-wedging, and ice blocks weakened by melting. The climber strives to be out of the couloir before the sun arrives, which means an early start to accomplish a round trip, an alternate route for the descent. . . .

Climbing in snow is often safest on ridges, where rock fall and avalanches are less likely but one is exposed to more wind and weather. The snow on ridges is sometimes partly "rotten ice," and outcroppings of rock form cornices that must be avoided. If there is lots of snow, ridges might be the only possibility on a long climb. Ridges are often easier to descend if a hasty retreat is necessary, and they are less sensitive to afternoon warming conditions that bring on avalanches and other falling debris.

16 | ON THE WALL —ONE WOMAN'S FIRST CLIMB

On the following pages you will see Heidi DeLay, who had never before attempted to climb a rock face. In one day, with three hours of instructions and a belay by a local guide, she succeeded in getting up a 200-foot granite face of about 5.3 difficulty in the Shawangunks. We started early on a foggy morning, covering the harness, knots, handholds, jams, balance, laybacks, friction climbing on a sloped surface, and rappelling techniques. After lunch, a rest and a three-quarter-mile walk, we made a 45-minute climb, which you see recorded here in time sequence. Heidi began below tree level and climbed out above.

Scary overhang a mile above the valley.

Working back up and around the ridge to her left.

Using a fingerjam,
squeezing,
and friction.

Bridging on all four points
on slack rope.

Feet not secure, but
good handholds are available.

Traversing to
ridge edge is
good strategy.

In high wind, footholds
seem fragile.

Appendixes

Some Places to Go for Equipment

ALASKA

Alaska Mountaineering &
  Hiking
2635 Spenard Rd.
Anchorage   99503

Alaska Mountaineering Co.
Talkertna   99676

CALIFORNIA

Granite Stairway
  Mountaineering
2160 University Ave.
Berkeley   94704

The North Face
2804 Telegraph Ave.
Berkeley   94705

Robbins Mountain Shop
7257 N. Abby Rd.
Fresno   93710

Kelty Mountaineering
1801 Victory Blvd.
Glendale   91201

Sport Chalet
951 Foothill Blvd.
La Canada   91011

Sports & Trails
1491 W. Whittier Blvd.
La Habra   90631

Robbins Mountain Shop
1508 10th St.
Modesto   95354

Stanley Andrews, Sporting
  Goods
443 12th Ave.
San Diego   92101

Granite Stairway
  Mountaineering
871 Santa Rosa Ave.
San Luis Obispo   93401

Granite Stairway
  Mountaineering
3040 State St.
Santa Barbara   93105

Granite Stairway
  Mountaineering
5425 Reseda Blvd.
Tarzana   91356

Pack & Piton
1252 W. Foothill Blvd.
Upland   91786

COLORADO

The Boulder Mountaineer
1329 Broadway
Boulder   80302

Lowe Alpine Systems, Inc.
1752 N. 55th St.
Boulder   80302

Neptune Mountaineering
1750 30th St.
Boulder   80301

Forrest Mountaineering,
   Ltd.
1517 Platte St.
Denver   80202

Mountain
938 S. Monaco Pkwy.
Denver   80224

The Mountain Shop
126 W. Laurel
Fort Collins   80521

Mount Chalet
140 W. 29th St.
Pueblo   81008

CONNECTICUT

Clapp & Treat
672 Farmington Ave.
West Hartford   06119

IDAHO

Sawtooth Mountaineering
5200 Fairview Ave.,
   Mini-Mall
Boise   83704

ILLINOIS

Erewhon Mountain Supply
1252 W. Devon Ave.
Chicago   60660

MASSACHUSETTS

Eastern Mountain Sports/
   Bargain Basement
1041 Commonwealth Ave.
Boston   02215

MINNESOTA

Midwest Mountaineering
309 Cedar Ave., South
Minneapolis   55454

MONTANA

Mountain Craft Equipment
659 Main St.
Billings   59102

Expeditions
   International/Bitterroot
   Backcountry Store
Box 1040
215 Main St.
Hamilton   59840

Base Camp
334 N. Jackson St.
Helena   59601

NEW HAMPSHIRE

Stephensons
R.F.D. #4
Gilford   03246

International Mountain
    Equipment
Paul Ross
Box 494
Main St.
North Conway   03860

Skimeister Ski Shop
Main St.
North Woodstock   03262

NEW YORK

Nippenose Equipment
215 N. Cayuga, Dewitt Mall
Ithaca   14850

Nippenose Equipment
3006 Erie Blvd., East
Syracuse   13224

OREGON

Recreational Sports
    Warehouse
311 Madison Ave., SW
Corvallis   97330

PENNSYLVANIA

Nippenose Equipment
225 W. Fourth St.
Williamsport   17701

UTAH

Timberline Sports, Inc.
3155 S. Highland Dr.
Salt Lake City   84106

WASHINGTON

Der Sportsmann
837 Front St.
Leavenworth   98826

North Face
501 E. Pine St.
Seattle   98122

Recreational Equipment,
    Inc.
1525 11th Ave.
Seattle   98122

Swallow's Nest
3320 Meridian Ave., North
Seattle   98103

Selkirk Bergsport
30 W. International Way
Spokane   99201

Asplund's Ski Touring
1544 N. Wenatchee Ave.
Wenatchee   98801

WISCONSIN

Erewhon Mountain Supply
State and Gorham Sts.
Madison   53703

WYOMING

Cross Country
    Mountaineering
128 W. Second St.
Casper   82601

Teton Mountaineering
Main Square
P.O. Box 1533
Jackson   83001

Rocky Mountaineering
211 Second St.
Laramie   82070

Some Places to Go to Find Other Hikers and Climbers

UNITED STATES

Coast-to-Coast

The National Audubon Society
  Headquarters: 1130 Fifth Ave., New York, N.Y. 10028.
  Western regional office: Sacramento, Calif.
  Nationwide: 375 branches and affiliates.
The Sierra Club
  Headquarters: 1050 Mills Tower, 270 Bush St., San
    Francisco, Calif. 94104. Offices in New York and
    Washington, D.C.
  Chapters in the following states (see listings under each):
    Arizona, California (11 chapters), Colorado, Illinois,
    Michigan, Nevada, New Mexico, New York, Oregon,
    Texas, Washington, D.C., and Wisconsin.

Regional

The Appalachian Trail Conference, 1718 N St., N.W.,
  Washington, D.C. 20036.
The Federation of Western Outdoor Clubs, Rte. 3, P.O.
  Box 172, Carmel, Calif. 93921.
The New England Trail Conference, 26 Bedford Terrace,
  Northampton, Mass. 01060.
The New York and New Jersey Trail Conference, P.O. Box
  2250, New York, N.Y. 10001.

Alaska

South Eastern Alaska Mountaineering Assoc., P.O. Box
  1314, Ketchikan 99901.

Arizona

Sierra Club: Grand Canyon Chapter, 555 W. Catalina Dr.,
  Phoenix 85013.

South Arizona Hiking Club, P.O. Box 12122, Tucson 85711.

California

Berkeley Hiking Club, P.O. Box 147, Berkeley 94701.

California Alpine Club, 244 Pacific Bldg., San Francisco 94103.

Contra Costa Hills Club, 306 Fortieth St., Rm. 3, Oakland 94609.

Desomount Club, 30711 S. Ganado Dr., Palos Verdes Peninsula 90274.

Federation of Western Outdoor Clubs, Rte. 3, P.O. Box 172, Carmel 93921.

Roamer Hiking Club, 3533 W. 74th Place, Inglewood 90305.

San Antonio Club, 750 S. Chapel Ave., Alhambra 91801.

Sierra Club

  Headquarters: 1050 Mills Tower, 270 Bush St., San Francisco 94104.

  Chapters: Los Angeles, Kern-Kaweah, Loma Prieta, Los Padres, Mother Lode, Redwood, Riverside, San Diego, Tehipite, Ventura, San Francisco Bay.

Tamalpais Conservation Club, 735 Pacific Bldg., San Francisco 94103.

Colorado

Colorado Mountain Club, 1400 Josephine St., Denver 80206

The Wilderness Society: Western Office, 2422 S. Downing St., Denver 80209.

Delaware

Brandywine Valley Outing Club, P.O. Box 7033, Wilmington 19803.

Wilmington Trail Club, P.O. Box 1184, Wilmington 19899.

District of Columbia

Alpine Information, Box 4875, Washington, D.C. 20008
The Appalachian Trail Conference, 1718 N St., N.W.,
   Washington 20036.
Potomac Appalachian Trail Club, 1718 N St., N.W., Wash-
   ington 20036.
The Wilderness Society, 729 Fifteenth St., N.W., Washing-
   ton 20005.

Georgia

Georgia Appalachian Trail Club, 4850 Northland Dr.,
   N.E., Atlanta 30305.

Hawaii

Hawaiian Trail and Mountain Club, P.O. Box 2238, Honolulu 96804.

Idaho

Idaho Alpine Club, P.O. Box 2885, Idaho Falls 83401.

Illinois

The Prairie Club, Rm. 1010, 38 S. Dearborn St., Chicago
   60603.

Indiana

Alpine Club of Canada, Midwest USA section: See Canada.

Iowa

Iowa Mountaineers, P.O. Box 163, Iowa City 52240.

Kentucky

Louisville Hiking Club, 2112 Eastview Ave., Louisville
   40205.

Maine

Maine Appalachian Trail Club, Kents Hill   04349.

Maryland

Maryland Appalachian Trail Club, 945 W. Washington St., Hagerstown   21740.
Mountain Club of Maryland, Inc., 280 Roundhill Rd., Ellicott City   21043.
Wanderbird Hiking Club, 6604 Wells Pkwy., University Park, Maryland   20782.

Massachusetts

Appalachian Mountain Club, 5 Joy St., Boston   02108.

Missouri

Missouri Walk-Ways Assoc., 613 Locust St., St. Louis 63101.

Montana

Montana Wilderness Assoc., P.O. Box 548, Bozeman 59715.
Rocky Mountaineers, 2100 South Ave., West, Missoula 59801

Nebraska

Omaha Walking Club, 5238 S. 22nd St., Omaha   68107.

New Hampshire

Appalachian Mountain Club: See Massachusetts.
Wonalancet Outdoor Club, Wonalancet   03897.

New Jersey

New York and New Jersey Trail Conference: See New York.

Philadelphia Trail Club, 205 S. Marion Ave., Wenonah 08090.

Torrey Botanical Club, Douglass College, New Brunswick 08901.

Union County Hiking Club, 508 Lincoln Ave., Cranford 07016.

Woodland Trail Walkers, 142 Lake Ave., Clifton 07011.

New York

Adirondack Mountain Club, Gabriels 12939.

Alpine Club of Canada, Eastern USA section: See Canada.

American Alpine Club, 113 E. 90th St. New York 10028.

American Youth Hostels, 14 W. 8th St., New York 10011.

Buffalo Hiking Club, Conservation Forum, Buffalo Museum of Science, Buffalo 14211.

Cayuga Trails Club, 133 Fayette St., Ithaca 14850.

The Finger Lakes Trail Conference, 2783 Brighton–Henrietta Town Rd., Rochester 14607.

Foothills Trails Club, R.F.D. #1, Fish Hill Rd., South Wales 14139.

Genesee Valley Hiking Club, Rochester Museum of Arts and Sciences, Rochester.

National Campers and Hikers Assoc., 7172 Transit Rd., Buffalo 14221.

The New York and New Jersey Trail Conference, P.O. Box 2250, New York 10001.

New York Hiking Club, 7825 Fourth Ave., Brooklyn 11209.

New York Ramblers, 97–37 Sixty-third Rd., Rego Park 11374.

Sierra Club, New York Office: 15 E. 53rd St., New York 10022; Atlantic Chapter: 445 Park Ave., New York 10022.

Taconic Hiking Club, 30 Continental Ave., Cohoes 12047.

Tramp and Trail Club, 62 E. 9th St., New York 10003.

Triple Cities Hiking Club, 95 Lisle Rd., Owego 13827.

Wanderbirds, 556 Fairview Ave., Brooklyn 11237.
Westchester Trails Assoc., 135 St. Pauls Place, New
  Rochelle 10801.

North Carolina

Carolina Mountain Club, P.O. Box 68, Asheville 28802.
Piedmont Appalachian Trail Club, 3513D Parkwood Dr.,
  Greensboro 27403.

Ohio

American Walkers Assoc., 6221 Robison Rd., Cincin-
  nati 45213.
Central Ohio Hiking Club, YMCA, 40 Long St.,
  Columbus 43215.
Cleveland Hiking Club, 3400 Archwood Ave.,
  Cleveland 44109.

Oregon

Alpine Club of Canada, Western USA section: See Canada.
Angoras, P.O. Box 12, Astoria 97103.
Chemeketans, 360½ State St., Salem 97301.
Desert Rats, Richland 97870.
Hood River Crag Rats, Hood River 97031.
Mazamas, 909 Nineteenth Ave. N.W., Portland 97209.
Obsidians, Inc., P.O. Box 322, Eugene 97401.
Trails Club of Oregon, P.O. Box 1243, Portland 97207.

Pennsylvania

Allentown Hiking Club, 722½ N. 12th St., Allentown
  18101.
Blue Mountain Eagle Climbing Club, 1020 Martin St.,
  Lebanon 17042.
Hiking Club of Lancaster, 601 West End Ave., South, Lan-
  caster 17603.
Horse-Shoe Trail Club, 1600 Three Penn Center Plaza,
  N.W., Philadelphia 19102.

Keystone Trails Assoc., P.O. Box 144, Concordville 19331.

Nature Hiking Club of Philadelphia (Batona), 144 Duffield St., Willow Grove   19090.

Susquehanna Appalachian Trail Club, 1412 Market St., Harrisburg   17103.

Williamsport Alpine Club, 1506 Almond St., Williamsport   17701.

York Hiking Club, 1957 Woodstream Dr., York   17402.

Tennessee

Cumberlands Hiking Club, 302 Old Mountain Rd., Chattanooga   37409.

Smoky Mountains Hiking Club, 201 South Purdue, Oak Ridge   37830.

Tennessee Eastman Hiking Club, % Tennessee Eastman Recreation Club, Bldg. 54D, Tennessee Eastman Co., Kingsport North   37662.

Tri-State Hiking Club, 1701 McCallie Ave., Chattanooga   37404.

Utah

Wasatch Mountain Club, 425 S. 8th West, Salt Lake City 84104.

Vermont

The Green Mountain Club, Inc., 108 Merchants Row, Rutland   05701.

Virginia

Mount Rogers Appalachian Trail Club, R.F.D. #1, Abingdon   24210.

Natural Bridge Appalachian Trail Club, 1608 Belfield Pl., Lynchburg   24503.

Roanoke Appalachian Trail Club, 2527 Churchill Dr., N.W., Roanoke   24012.

Shenandoah-Rockfish Appalachian Trail Club, P.O. Box 344, Scottsville   24590.

Washington

Alpine Roamers, Wenatchee   98801.
Cascadians, Yakima   98901.
Hobnailers, P.O. Box 1074, Spokane   99210.
Klahhane Club, P.O. Box 494, Port Angeles   98362.
Mount Baker Club, P.O. Box 73, Bellingham   98225.
Mount Saint Helens Club, P.O. Box 843, Longview 98632.
Mountaineers, Inc., P.O. Box 122, Seattle   98111.
Olympians, Inc., P.O. Box 401, Hoquiam   98550.
The Ptarmigans, P.O. Box 1821, Vancouver   98663.
Rimrock Mountaineers, Coulee Dam   99116.
Skagit Alpine Club, P.O. Box 513, Mount Vernon   98273.
Spokane Mountaineers, Inc., P.O. Box 1013, Spokane   99210.
Wanderers, 515 Floravista, Olympia   98501.
Washington Alpine Club, P.O. Box 352, Seattle   98111.

Wisconsin

Wisconsin Go-Hiking Club, 3863 N. 37th St., Milwaukee   53216.
Wisconsin Hoofers, The Wisconsin Union, 770 Langdon St., Madison   53703.

Wyoming

Wyoming Mountaineers, Casper   82601.

CANADA

Coast-to-Coast

The Alpine Club of Canada, 2974 W. 28th Ave., Vancouver 8, B.C.

Canadian Youth Hostels Assoc., National Office: 1406 W. Broadway, Vancouver 9, B.C.

Alberta

Canadian Youth Hostels Assoc.: Mountain Region, 455 Twelfth St., N.W., Calgary; Northwest Region, 10922 Eighty-eighth Ave., Edmonton.
Skyline Trail Hikers of the Canadian Rockies, 622 Madison Ave., S.W., Calgary

British Columbia

The Alpine Club of Canada, 2974 W. 28th Ave., Vancouver 8.
B.C. Mountaineering Club, P.O. Box 2674, Vancouver 9.
Canadian Youth Hostels Assoc.: Pacific Region, 1406 W. Broadway, Vancouver 9.
Island Mountain Ramblers, 440 Chestnut St., Nanaimo.
North Shore Hikers, % 1192 W. 26th Ave., Vancouver 9.
Simon Fraser University Outdoor Club, Burnaby.
Varsity Outdoor Club, University of British Columbia, Vancouver 8.

Nova Scotia

Canadian Youth Hostels Assoc.: Maritime Region, P.O. Box 2332, Halifax.

Ontario

The Bruce Trail Assoc., 33 Hardale Cres, Hamilton.
Canadian Youth Hostels Assoc.: Great Lakes Region, 86 Scollard St., Toronto 5.
National Campers and Hikers Assoc., 8 Thorpe Rd., Weston.
Niagara Escarpment Trail Council, P.O. Box 1, St. Catharines.
Toronto Hiking and Conservation Club, P.O. Box 121, Postal Station F, Toronto 5.

Walker Mineralogical Club of Toronto, 12 Redwing Pl., Don Mills.

Quebec

Canadian Youth Hostels Assoc.: Saint Lawrence Region, 754 Sherbrooke St., West, Montreal 2.

(Many universities have mountaineering clubs.)

Some Places to Go for Instruction

The Bob Culp Climbing
  School
1329 Broadway
Boulder, CO   80302
(303-442-8355)
(Rock climbing year round, ice climbing through early spring.)

Challenge/Discovery
P.O. Box 229
Crested Butte, CO   81224
(303-349-5432)
(Western wilderness course. Cross-country skiing, avalanche study, winter camping.)

Colorado Outward Bound
  School
945 Pennsylvania Ave.
Denver, CO   80203
(303-837-0880)

(Ski mountaineering, ice climbing, glissading, winter camp craft.)

Dartmouth Outward
  Bound School
P.O. Box 50
Hanover, NH   03755
(603-646-3359)
(Snowshoeing, alpine touring, winter camping in White Mountains and Connecticut lake regions of N.H.)

Eastern Mountain Sports
  Climbing School
P.O. Box 494
Main St.
North Conway, NH   03860
(603-356-5287)
or:

44 Vose Farm Rd.
Peterborough, NH   03458

(Stores in Boston, Denver,
St. Paul, Hartford,
Buffalo, Ardsley, Long
Island and New York
City.)

Geneva Spur Limited
1109 Lakewood Dr.
Vienna, VA   22180
(703–281–3316/3533)

(At Great Falls Park near
Washington, D.C., rock
climbing from beginning
to very advanced. Snow
and ice climbing classes
are also available.)

Great Plains
Mountaineering
% Richard Lapted
Wichita State University
1845 Fairmont
Wichita, KS   67208

Hurricane Island Outward
Bound School
P.O. Box 429
Rockland, ME   04841
(207–594–5548)

(Winter wilderness short
courses in Maine's
Mahoosuc Mountains.
Includes cross-country
skiing, snowshoeing, and
climbing.)

International Backpackers
Assoc. Inc.

P.O. Box 85
Lincoln Center,
ME   04458
(207–794–6062)

(Has annual Winter
Backpacking School.
Winter gear, cold weather
health concerns, special
foods, clothing and
environmental awareness
are covered.)

International School of
Mountaineering
Club Vagabond
1854 Leysin
Switzerland

Jackson Hole Mountain
Guides
Teton Village, WY   83025

Johann Mountain Guides
P.O. Box 19171
Portland, OR   97219
(503–244–7672)

(Weekend seminar in igloo
and snow cave building at
Mount Hood in northern
Oregon. Winter
mountaineering
techniques, ski touring
and snowshoeing.)

Mid-America Voyageurs
West Branch, IA   52358

(Teaches winter camping
and cross-country skiing
in Yellowstone and the

Tetons in December and
January. Six-day
program for people with
little or no winter travel
experience.)

Ted Mize
Mountain Explorers
Topeka, KS   66601

Mountain People School
157 Oak Spring Dr.
San Anselmo, CA   94960
(415–457–3664)
(Backpacking, rock
climbing, snowshoeing
instruction in the
California Sierra
Nevada.)

National Outdoor
Leadership School
P.O. Box AA
Lander, WY   82520
(307–733–5662)
(Twenty-six courses,
including camping, trail
technique, environment
mountaineering, fishing,
and expedition dynamics.
Includes Mexico, Alaska
and Africa. Some college
credits given.)

North Carolina Outward
Bound School
P.O. Box 817
Morgantown, NC   28655
(704–437–6112)

(A winter wilderness course
in North Carolina's
Pisgah National Forest.)

North Cascades Alpine
School
1212 24th AB
Bellingham,   WA
(206–671–1505)
(Climbs in Mexico to
18,701'.)

Northwest Outward Bound
School
0110 SW Bancroft St.
Portland, OR   97201
(503–243–1993)
(Teaches
ski-mountaineering,
including solo climbs, in
Oregon's Eagle Cap
Wilderness.)

Outdoor Experience
62 Rt. 22
Greenbrook, NJ   08812
(201–968–4344)
(Basic and intermediate
rock and ice climbing
instruction, cross-country
skiing and backpacking.)

Outdoor Leadership
Training Seminars
2220 Birch
Denver, CO   80207
(Ski touring, ski
mountaineering, summer

mountaineering, rock
climbing courses.)

Outward Bound School
945 Pennsylvania St.
Denver, CO   80203
(303–837–0880)

(Seven schools in the United
States; 34 schools on 5
continents serving 17
countries. Good technical
courses and training for
beginners.)

Palisade School of
Mountaineering
P.O. Box 694
Bishop, CA   93514
(714–935–4330)

(Winter climbing in
Scotland, British seacliff
climbing. Mountain
medicine, rock, snow and
ice climbing.)

Paul Ross Climbing School
P.O. Box 494
Main St.
North Conway, NH   03860
(603–356–5287)

Pop Hollandsworth
Mountaineering Instructor
Asheville School
Asheville, NC   28806

(Runs a three-week course
in summer in western
North Carolina.

Hollandsworth is a
former Outward Bound
instructor.)

Rock and Snow
44 Main St.
New Paltz, NY   12561

Rocky Mountain Climbing
School
P.O. Box 2432
Aspen, CO   81611

Southwest Outward Bound
School
P.O. Box 2840
Santa Fe, NM   87501
(505–988–5573)

(Short courses in
canyoneering, rock
climbing, desert survival.)

Sullivan Education
Ventures, SEV
3272 Alpine Rd.
Menlo Park, CA   94025

The Summer Ski
Pink Garter Plaza
Jackson, WY   83001
(307–733–5662)

(Backpacking guide service
and rentals)

Western Door Wilderness
School
172 "N" St.
Salt Lake City, UT
(801–322–5381)

(Twelve- and eighteen-day

desert backpacking courses in Utah's Canyonlands.)

Wilderness Challenge
P.O. Box 1313
Kent, WA   98031

(Mountaineering, basic rock climbing, all phases of wilderness living in Colorado.)

The Wilderness Institute, Inc.
333 Fairfax St.
Denver, CO   80220
(303–393–0400)

(Mountaineering courses in the Rocky Mountains.)

Also see: *The Climber's Sourcebook* ($4.95) by Anne Schneider and Steven Schneider (New York: Anchor Press/Doubleday 1976). This book lists schools, clubs, private secondary schools, camps, traveling camps, guided ascents, and courses.

Some Places to Go for Local Information

Adirondack Mountain Club	Gabriels, N.Y. N.Y.C., N.Y.
American Alpine Club	Boston, Mass.
Appalachian Mountain Club	Chapters throughout New England and in N.Y.C.
California Alpine Club	San Francisco, Calif.
Canadian Alpine Club	Vancouver; B.C.
Cascadians	Yakima, Wash.
Chicago Mountaineering Club	Chicago, Ill.
Colorado Mountain Club	Denver, Colo.
Dartmouth Mountaineering Club	Hanover, N.H.
Desert Rats	Richland, Ore.
Federation of Western Outdoor Clubs	Eugene, Ore.

Georgia Appalachian Trail Club	Atlanta, Ga.
Harvard Mountaineering Club	Cambridge, Mass.
Hood River Crag Rats	Hood River, Ore.
Inter Mountain Alpine Club	Richland, Wash.
Iowa Mountaineers	Iowa City, Ia.
Los Alamos Mountaineers	Los Alamos, N.M.
Mazamas	Portland, Ore.
Minnesota Rovers	Minneapolis, Minn.
M.I.T. Outing Club	Cambridge, Mass.
Mountaineers, Inc.	Seattle, Wash.
Obsidians, Inc.	Eugene, Ore.
Olympians, Inc.	Hoquiam, Wash.
Pittsburgh Climbers	Pittsburgh, Pa.
Potomac Appalachian Trail Club	Washington, D.C.
Rensselaer Mountaineering Club	Troy, N.Y.
Rimrock Mountaineers	Coulee Dam, Wash.
Sierra Club Has rock climbing section, desert peaks section	Chapters in San Diego, Los Angeles, Palo Alto– San Jose, Fresno, San Francisco
Smoky Mountains Hiking Club	Oak Ridge, Tenn.
Spokane Mountaineers, Inc.	Spokane, Wash.
Stanford Alpine Club	Stanford, Calif.
Trails Club of Oregon	Portland, Ore.
University of Oregon Alpine Club	Eugene, Ore.
University of Wyoming Outing Club	Laramie, Wyo.
Wasatch Mountain Club	Salt Lake City, Utah
Washington Alpine Club	Seattle, Wash.
Wisconsin Hoofers	Madison, Wis.
Wy'east Climbers	Portland, Ore.

Wyoming Mountaineers   Casper, Wyo.
Yale Mountaineering Club   New Haven, Conn.

Special Organizations for Advanced Experience

Alaska Mountain
  Expeditions
Ray Genet
Talkeetna, AK   99676
(907–733–2306)

(Wilderness,
  cross-country-ski and
  snowshoe treks.
  Mountain and glacier
  seminars.)

American Adventurers
  Association
Suite 404
5200 University Way, NE
Seattle, WA   98105

American Wilderness
  Experience, Inc.
P.O. Box 1486, No. 2D
Boulder, CO   80306
(303–449–0056)

(Wilderness horsepack,
  backpack, and
  hot-air-balloon treks in
  Colorado and Arizona.)

Aurora Borealis
  Expeditions

Box 20735
Minneapolis, MN   55420

(Ski-touring, canoeing and
  backpacking trips in
  remote wilderness areas
  throughout the United
  States and Canada.)

Avalanche
1794 N. Highland Rd.
Bethel Park, PA   15241
(412–833–7800)

(Four-day backpacking
  exploration of
  Assateague Island off the
  coast of Maryland.)

Baja's Frontier Tours
4365 New Jersey
San Diego, CA   92116
(714–299–1360)

(Custom and scheduled
  trips and expeditions in
  Baja, California and
  Mexico.)

Colorado Alpine Adventure
2424 S. Columbine
Denver, CO   80210

(Winter mountaineering, ice climbing, ski-touring.)

Fantasy Ridge Mountain Guides
P.O. Box 2106
Estes Park, CO   80517
(303–586–5758)

(Winter climbing, ski-mountaineering, ice climbing. Previous experience with anchoring, knots and belaying needed.)

L. D. Frome Outfitter
P.O. Box MM
Afton, WY   83110
(307–886–5240)

(Wyoming wilderness backpacking treks. Teton wilderness pack trips.)

In the Tracks of Fremont, Inc.
P.O. Box 346-M
Steamboat, NV   89436

(Emphasis on natural history, photography, participation and survival techniques. Winter and spring schedule to Mojave Desert and Death Valley.)

Infinite Odyssey
14A Union Park St.
Boston, MA   02118
(617–542–0060)

(Climbs of Mt. McKinley and in British Columbia and Mexico; kayaking in Alaska and Colorado, ski touring, bike touring, and wilderness canoeing.)

Jackson Hole Mountain Guides, Inc.
Teton Village, WY   83025
(307–733–4979)

(Complete educational programs in alpine mountaineering, guide service concessioned in Grand Teton. For every level of experience.)

Liberty Bell Alpine Tours
Mazama, WA   98833
(509–996–2250)

(Mountaineering courses, backpacking tours, helicopter skiing, and whitewater river trips.)

Lynx Track Winter Travel
5375 Eureka Rd.
P.O. Box MM
Excelsior, MN   55331
(612–474–5190)

(Dog sled/ski tour courses and expeditions in Minnesota-Canada boundary waters wilds.)

Mt. Adams Wilderness Institute
Flying L Ranch

Glenwood, WA   98619
(509–364–3511)

(Wilderness/glacier travel, snow, rock, and ice climbing on huge glaciated Cascade volcano.)

Rocky Mountain Expeditions
P.O. Box 1
Buena Vista, CO   81211
(303–395–8466)

(Cross-country ski trips, snow caves or cabins.)

Eric Rybacks — Horizons Unlimited
P.O. Box 147
Pocatello, ID   83201
(208–233–9428)

(Mountaineering, backpacking, rock climbing school. Courses or guided tours in the Idaho primitive area.)

Sourdough Outfitters
Bettles, AK   99726
(907–692–5252)

(Canoeing, backpacking, dogsledding, ski touring, fishing and photography in Alaska's Central Brooks Range.)

Trans Montane Outfitters, Ltd.
215 W. Brook Run Dr.
Richmond, VA   23233
(804–784–3615)

(Backpacking treks in the East.)

Women in the Wilderness
San Francisco Ecology Center
13 Columbus Ave.
San Francisco, CA   94111
(415–982–4588)

(Seasonal newsletters list a calendar of classes, events in the outdoors from one to thirty days' length — all directed to women's special interests.)

Yellowstone Wilderness Guides
P.O. Box 446M
Red Lodge, MT   59068
(406–446–2636)

(Guided backpack trips in Absaroka, Bear Tooth and Yellowstone wilderness areas.)

International Guides

Adventure Center
5540-A College Ave.
Oakland, CA   94618
(415–654–1879)

(Worldwide adventure
   travel, 8–114 days.)

Arnica Adventure Ltd.
   Canada
RR #1
Nelson, B.C.   V1L5P4
Canada

(Backpacking, canoeing,
   and wilderness travel in
   British Columbian
   Kootenays.)

Encounter Overland
   Expeditions
369 Pine St. #516
San Francisco, CA   94104
(415–421–7199)

(Experienced organizers of
   rugged camping
   expeditions in Africa,
   Asia, South America.)

Goway Ventures
Suite 101
53 Yonge St.
Toronto, Ont.
Canada
(416–863–0799)

(Three weeks to four
   months in South-Central
   America.)

High Country Passage
P.O. Box 879
La Porte, CO   80535
(303–221–2834)

(Two- and three-week treks
   through Guatemala.
   Previous hiking
   experience needed.)

Himalaya
3023 Franklin St.
San Francisco, CA   94123
(415–441–2933)

(Trekking and wilderness
   expeditions to Kashmir,
   Ladakh, Nepal.)

International Treks and
   Travel
1005 Maplehurst Pk. SW,
   No. 2
Knoxville, TN   37902

(Treks in Kashmir and
   Ladakh, northern India.)

The Iowa Mountaineers,
   Inc.
30 Prospect Pl.
P.O. Box 163
Iowa City, IA   52240
(319–337–7163)

(Mountain outings/
   expeditionary
   sponsorship in U.S.,
   Canada, Peru, Europe,
   East Africa, New Zealand.

Superb rock climbing and cross-country skiing and winter survival courses.)

Journeys
P.O. Box 7545
Ann Arbor, MI 48107
(313-995-4617)

(Trips to Arun Valley, Ganesh Himal, Mt. Everest, Nepal; Kashmir/Ladakh; Sri Lanka; Colombia.)

Kashmir Mountain Travel
E-13 Kalindi
New Delhi 110014 India

(Specializes in outfitting and guiding groups.)

Mountain Travel, Inc.
Albany, CA 94706
(415-527-8100)

(International river rafting, desert caravans, country walks, mountaineering. Climbs in the Peruvian Andes and around the world. Each expedition is made up of eight to fifteen people and led by a well-known explorer.)

Northern Lights Alpine Recreation
P.O. Box 399
Invermere, B.C. VOA 1KO
Canada
(604-342-6042)

(Day tours, snowshoe treks, glacier tours and winter mountaineering in the Canadian Rockies through April.)

Ptarmigan Tours
% Repp Agencies
290 Wallinger
Kimberley, B.C.
Canada
(604-427-3510)

(Through Purcell Range of southeastern British Columbia, including the Bugaboos.

REI Adventure Travel
1525 Eleventh Ave.
Seattle, WA 98122
(206-322-7800)

(Expeditions to spots around the world, including Norway, Himalayan foothills, New Zealand.)

The Sherpa Co-operative
P.O. Box 1338
Katmandu, Nepal

(Specialists in planning treks and expeditions.)

Sherpa Expeditions
3 Bedford Rd.
London W4 1JD
England

(Adventures in the Himalayas.)

272 | APPENDIXES

South American Wilderness
   Adventures
1760-M Solano
Berkeley, CA   94707
(415–524–5111)
(Trekking expeditions,
   wildlife and natural
   history tours, jungle
   explorations and
   anthropology tours to
   remote areas of Peru,
   Ecuador, Bolivia,
   Patagonia and Galapagos
   Islands.)

Tropical Ice (Mountain
   Guides)
Iain Allan and Vince Fayad

P.O. Box 57341
Nairobi, Kenya

(Professionally guided trips
   in the mountains of East
   Africa—vacations for the
   walker and the technical
   climber.)

Ven-Turs
P.O. Box 493
Woodinville, WA   98072
(Trips to Venezuela's
   Roraima region.)

Wilderness World
1342 Jewell
Pacific Grove, CA   93950
(408–373–5882)

Recommended Reading List

The following is interesting reading for women who have had beginner's experience in the field. You should know that there is no shortage of books on climbing subjects. Mountain climbers have written more about their experiences and craft than any other sportspeople in any field, with the possible exception of fishermen.

BOOKS

ABC of Avalanche Safety. Edward R. LaChapelle.
Accidents in North America Mountaineering. The American Alpine Club.
Advanced First Aid for All Outdoors. Peter F. Eastman, M.D.
Advanced Rockcraft. Royal Robbins.
Age of Mountaineering, The. James Ramsey Ullman.
American Red Cross, First Aid Manuals.
Among the Alps with Bradford. Bradford Washburn.

Annapurna: The First Conquest of an Eight Thousand Meter Peak. Maurice Herzog.
Ascent of Denali, The. Hudson Stuck.
Ascent of K2. Ardito Desio.

Banner in the Sky. James Ramsey Ullman.
Basic River Canoeing. Robert E. McNair.
Basic Rockcraft. Royal Robbins.
Belaying the Leader. Richard W. Leonard & Arnold Wexler.
Butcher, The: The Ascent of Yerupaja. John Sack.

Call of the Snowy Hispar, The. Fanny Bullock Workman & William Hunter Workman.
Camera in the Hills, A. Frank S. Smythe.
Canoeing. American National Red Cross.
Le Cervin. Charles Gos.
Climber's Guide to the Olympics. Olympic Mountain Rescue.
Climbing Ice. Yvon Chouinard.
Climbing in Britain. J. E. Q. Barford.
Climbs in the Canadian Rockies. Frank S. Smythe.
Complete Book of Fly Fishing, The. Joe Brooks.
Complete Mountaineer, The. George D. Abraham.
Conquest of Everest, The. Sir John Hunt.

Diet for a Small Planet. Frances Moore Lappe.

Ecology. Eugene P. Odum.
Endurance. Sir Ernest Shackelton.
Everest—The Hard Way. Chris Bonington.

Face Nord. Saint Loup.
Field Biology and Ecology. C. Smith.
Freedom of the Hills. The Mountaineers.
Frostbite. Bradford Washburn.

Geology Illustrated. John S. Shelton.
Glaciers. Robert Sharp.
Grande Crevasse, La. Roger Frison-Roche.

Hall of the Mountain King, The. Howard H. Snyder.
Handbook of American Mountaineering. Kenneth Henderson.

High Adventure. Bob Spring & Ira Spring.
History of Mountaineering in the Alps, A. Claire Elaine Engel.
Hours of Exercise in the Alps. John Tyndall.
Hypothermia—Killer of the Unprepared. Dr. Ted Lathrop.

Igloo Building. Reprint of article in *Off Belay* magazine.
International Everest Expedition, The. Murray Sayle, *Life,* July 2, 1972.
International Mountain Rescue Handbook. Hamish MacInnes.
In the Throne Room of the Mountain Gods. Galen Rowell.

Journal of a Trapper. Osborne Russell.
Journals of Lewis and Clark, The. Edited by Bernard De Voto.

Kanchenjunga Climbed. Charles Evans.
Killer Mountain, Nanga Parbat, The. Karl M. Herrligkoffer.
Kingdom of Adventures, Everest. James Ramsey Ullman.
Knots for Mountaineering. Phil D. Smith.
K2, The Savage Mountain. Charles M. Houston & Robert H. Bates.

Master of Rock. Pat Ament.
Matterhorn, The. Guido Rey.
Medicine for Mountaineering. Edited by James A. Wilkerson.
Men, Women and Mountains. Sir Claud Schuster.
Modern Rope Techniques in Mountaineering. Bill March.
Mountain Conquest. Eric E. Shipton & Bradford Washburn.
Mountain Craft. Geoffrey Winthrop Young.
Mountaineering. C. T. Dent.
Mountaineering. Edited by Sidney Spencer.
Mountaineering: The Freedom of the Hills. Peggg Ferber, ed.
Mountaineering First Aid: A Guide to Accident Response and First Aid Care, 2d ed. Dick Mitchell.
Mountaineering Log Book. Nelson & Johnson.
Mountaineering Medicine: A Wilderness Medical Guide. Fred T. Darvill, Jr.
Mountaineering: The Freedom of the Hills. Harvey Manning.
Mountain Medicine: A Clinical Study of Cold and High Altitudes. Michael Ward.

Mountain Medicine and Physiology. Mountain Medicine Symposium.

Mountain of the Storms. Andy Harvard & Todd Thompson.

Mountain Photography. C. Douglas Milner.

Mountain Search and Rescue Operations. Grand Teton Assoc.

Mountain Search for the Lost Victim. Dennis Kelley.

Mountains with a Difference. Geoffrey Winthrop Young.

Mountain Way, The. R. L. G. Irving.

Mountain World, The. Swiss Foundation for Alpine Research.

My Climbs in the Alps and Caucasus. Albert F. Mummery.

Nanga Parbat Pilgrimage. Hermann Buhl.

NOLS Cookery. Nancy Pallister.

North Wall, A Novel. Roger Hubank.

On Climbing. Charles Evan.

148 F. Art Davidson.

On High Hills, Geoffrey Winthrop Young.

On Ice and Snow and Rock. Gaston Rebuffat.

Peaks, Passes and Glaciers. Edited by John Ball.

Playground of Europe, The. Sir Leslie Stephen.

Postscript to Adventure. Sir Claud Schuster.

Premier de Cordée. Roger Frison-Roche.

Rock for Climbing. C. Douglas Milner.

Romance of Mountaineering, The. R. L. G. Irving.

Scrambles Amongst the Alps. Edward Whymper.

Snowshoeing. Gene Prater.

South Col. Wilred Noyce.

Splendid Wayfaring, The. John A. Neihardt.

Tents in the Clouds: The First Women's Himalayan Expedition. Monica Jackson & Elizabeth Stark.

Tiger of the Snows. Tenzing Norgay As Told to James Ramsey Ullman.

Trout. Ray Bergman & Edward C. Janes.

Ultimate Athlete, The. George Leonard.

Weather. Lehr, Burnett & Herbert S. Zim.
White Tower, The. James Ramsey Ullman.
Wie Die Schweizer Alpen Erobert Warden. Dr. Max Senger.
Wilderness Emergencies (Surviving the Unexpected). Gene Fear.
Wilderness Handbook, The. Paul Petzoldt.

The American Alpine Club has a master library at 113 E. 90th St., New York, NY 10028, which is open to the public. It also has branches in Jackson Hole, the Teton County Library, the Denver Public Library, the Yosemite Research Center (in Yosemite National Park), and the offices of the Mountaineers in Seattle, Washington. The Malibu Public Library in California will have a branch by 1980.

MAGAZINES

Adventure Travel
Suite 301
444 Ravenna Blvd., NE
Seattle, WA   98115

American Alpine Journal
13 E. 90th St.
New York, NY   10028

Backpacking Journal
229 Park Ave., South
New York, NY   10003

Backpacker Magazine
55 Adams St.
Bedford, NY   10507

Better Camping
Woodall's Publishing Co.
500 Hyacinth Pl.
Highland Park, IL   60035

Camping Journal
Davis Publications

229 Park Ave., South
New York, NY   10003

Climbing
P.O. Box E
Aspen, CO   81611

The Conservationist
New York State Dept. of
    Environmental
    Conservation
Albany, NY   12204

The Explorers Journal
Explorers Club
46 E. 70th St.
New York, NY   10021

Friends of the Earth
124 Spear St.
San Francisco, CA   94105

The Geographical Magazine
1 Kensington Gore

London SW7 2AR
England

Jackson Hole and the Tetons
High Altitude Graphics,
Inc.
P.O. Box 112
Teton Village, WY   83025

*Jackson Hole, the Tetons, and
Yellowstone*
High Country Services
P. O. Box 2058
Jackson, WY   83001

Mariah
3401 W. Division St.
Chicago, IL   60651

Mountain
Mountain Magazine, Ltd.
3 Edgedale Rd.
Sheffield 7
England

Mountain Gazette
745 Walnut St.
Boulder, CO   80302

*Mountain Safety Research
Newsletter*
S. 96th St. at 8th Ave.,
South
Seattle, WA   98108

*National Outdoor Leadership
School Alumni Magazine*
P.O. Box AA
Lander, WY   82520

National Wildlife Magazine
National Wildlife
Membership Services

1412 Sixteenth St., NW
Washington, DC   20036

*Off Belay, The Mountain
Magazine*
15630 SE 124th St.
Renton, WA   98055

Outdoor Women
919 N. Michigan Ave.,
Station 3310
Chicago, IL   60611
or
500 Twelfth St., SW, Station
810
Washington, DC   20024

Outside
Straight Arrow Publications
745 Fifth Ave.
New York, NY   10022
Editorial offices:
625 Third St.
San Francisco, CA   94107

Outward Bound News
165 W. Putnam Ave.
Greenwich, CT   06830

Search and Rescue Magazine
P.O. Box 153
Montrose, CA   91020

Sierra Club Magazine
530 Bush St.
San Francisco, CA   94108

Ski Magazine
380 Madison Ave.
New York, NY   10017

Skiing
Ziff Davis Publishing Co.
1 Park Ave.
New York, NY   10016

Sports Illustrated
Rockefeller Center
New York, NY   10020

Summit
P.O. Box 1889
Big Bear Lake, CA   92315

Teton Magazine
P.O. Box 1903
Jackson, WY   83001

Wilderness Camping
1597 Union St.
Schenectady, NY   12309

GLOSSARY

I have included in the glossary not only terms found in this book, but others that you will encounter as you get into more advanced climbing.

Abseil. *See* Rappel.

Aid-climbing. Climbing with the use of slings, ropes, nuts, pitons, etc., for physical assistance as well as for safety.

Alpine. A climbing route with a combination of technical rock, snow, and ice.

Anchor. An attachment to rock, snow or ice, using a sling, nut or other device(s). In particular, the attachment used to secure the belayer.

Arête. A sharp, narrow mountain ridge leading up to the summit.

Arrest (also self-arrest). An essential technique for stopping a slip or fall on snow, ice or slippery grass, using the ice axe as a brake.

Ascender. A mechanical device used in climbing a rope.

Belay. To secure a rope around a rock or other anchorage in such a way as to make fast the climber to the stance.

Bivouac. Overnight stay on a mountain with a minimum of equipment.

Bolt. An anchor placed in a hole drilled for that purpose in the rock.

Buttress. A mass of rock projecting from the mountain, on which one usually finds rock-climbing routes.

Carabiner (or snap link). A steel or alloy oval with a one-way gate in one side, used for attaching the rope to a belay or harness.

Chimney. A narrow gully that is wide enough to bridge and is usually vertical.

Chimneying (or backing up or bridging). A way of ascending a wide crack with one's back pressed against one wall and one's feet against the other.

Chockstone. A rock or stone that is jammed into a crack so tightly that a rope can be threaded behind it for a belay.

Chure. A steep, narrow gap extending down a face, into which avalanches and rockfall are likely to be channeled.

Cirque. A glacier confined to its place of origin, either because it has not gathered enough mass to move on or because it has retreated for a previously greater extension. Also the basin or lake created by such a glacier.

Col. *See* Saddle.

Combined tactics. A method in which the second climber lets herself be used as a ladder in order to allow the leader to surmount an obstacle.

Corner. A vertical, angular feature, usually 90 degrees.

Cornice. An overhanging mass of snow at the crest of a ridge.

Couloir. Concave rock face.

Crack. A narrow chimney too small to fit the body, but into which an arm, hand or foot can be wedged.

Crampons. Metal frames with spikes protruding from the bottoms, made to be strapped onto the climber's boots and to bite into ice or snow, thus enabling her to ascend steep slopes without cutting steps or increasing her security in steps.

Crevasse. A deep crack in the ice of a glacier caused by the stress of the glacier's movement over uneven ground.

Diff. An abbreviation for the term difficult, a degree of rigor in rock climbing.

Étrier. A short rope ladder used in artificial aid-climbing.

Exposure. A climb is said to be exposed when it is difficult and when there is lots of daylight beneath it.

Face. A steep, broad side of a mountain. A mountain may have several faces with ridges or buttresses in between. A face generally refers to a mountainside at least steep enough to present serious climbing difficulties.

Free-climbing. A type of climbing in which slings, nuts, pitons, etc., are used only to protect the climber in case of a fall, not for aid in climbing.

Gardening. The process of cleaning out a route to find the holds.

Gendarme. A tower or pinnacle dominating a ridge and obstructing progress.

Glacier. A mass of snow and ice that moves slowly down a mountainside or valley.

Glissade. A method of descending snowfields by sliding.

Gully. A gorge on the mountainside, surrounded by steeper rocks and generally having a stream in it.

Horn. A protruding piece of rock over which a sling can be hung for an anchor.

Icefall. A mass of jumbled ice produced from a steep section in the glacial bed.

Jam crack. A more or less vertical crack that is climbed by wedging or jamming different parts of the body into it and pulling up on them.

Jammed holds. A way of wedging a hand, finger or fist into a crack to get a grip.

Knife edge. A sharp ridge crest with precipitous exposure on both sides.

Knitting. A quantity of tangled climbing rope.

Layback. A strenuous technique for climbing a crack. The hands pull while the legs push.

Leader. The first person on the rope.

Mixed climbing. In classical mountaineering, the term refers to any climbing that involves rock, snow and ice. It also refers to alternating free-climbing and direct aid, especially in pure rock climbing.

Moraine. A heap of rock that has been or is being carried by a glacier.

Nail. To ascend cracks with the use of pitons.

Nut. Metal chock or block—sometimes an actual mechanic's nut—that can be attached to wires, slings, etc.

Peel-off. Fall or jump off a climb.

Pitch. The distance or route from one belay stance to the next. It could be a full rope length or it could be much less.

Piton (or peg). A metal spike with a hole in it or a ring attached. It can be pounded into rock cracks or into ice for use as a belay.

Rappel. A fast method of descending a mountain or cliff by sliding down a doubled rope that is wrapped around the body in such a way as to produce enough friction to control descent.

Rib. A small ridge of bare rock.

Roof. An overhanging rock formation that may extend out anywhere from a few feet to dozens of feet.

Rope. Mountaineering ropes, now generally made of nylon, except for some special-purpose ropes.

Running belay (or runner). A device for safeguarding the leader. The rope runs through a carabiner attached to a sling belay.

Saddle (or col). A pass or gap between two peaks.

Sérac. Block or tower of ice.

Slab. Flat section of rock lying at an angle less than perpendicular to the ground.

Slack. Any non-tense rope between two climbers.

Sling. A loop of rope or webbing.

Stance. A place where a climber can belay herself and bring up the next person.

Stirrups. Direct-aid slings that are like rope ladders with aluminum rungs.

Traverse. A section of a route that crosses a cliff or face horizontally.

Wall. A steep cliff or face that is vertical or almost vertical.

BIBLIOGRAPHY

Anderson, Bob. *Stretching.* (There is an excellent wall chart which can be obtained by sending $2.00 to Bob Anderson, Stretching, P.O. Box 2734, Fullerton, CO 92633.)

Blair, Clay, Jr. *Survive.* New York: Berkeley, 1973.

Blum, Arlene. "Triumph and Tragedy on Annapurna." *National Geographic,* Vol. 155, #3, March 1979.

Bohach, Carol M., and Martin, Susan. *Luxury in a Tent.* New York: Playboy Press, 1977.

Bonney, Orrin H., and Lorraine. *Field Book Wind River Range.* Houston: Orrin H. Bonney & Lorraine G. Bonney, 1968.

Boy Scout Handbook. North Brunswick, N.J.: Boy Scouts of America, 1962.

Brower, David (ed.). *The Sierra Club Manual of Ski Mountaineering.* San Francisco: A Sierra Club–Ballantine book, 1962.

Bunnelle, Hasse, with Thomas, Winnie. *Food for Knapsackers: And Other Trail Travelers.* San Francisco: Sierra Club Books, 1971.

Carter, H. Adams. *American Alpine Journal.* New York: The American Alpine Journal, 1971.

Dillard, Annie. *Pilgrim at Tinker Creek.* New York: Harper's Magazine Press, 1974.

Disley, John. *Tackle Climbing.* London: Stanley Paul & Co., first ed. 1959, rev. ed. 1977.

Fletcher, Colin. *The Complete Walker.* New York: Alfred A. Knopf, 1971.

Forsdyke, A. G. *Knowledge Through Color, Weather and Weather Forecasting*. New York: Grosset & Dunlap, 1970.

Freuchen, Peter. *Book of the Eskimos*. New York: Fawcett Premier Books, 1961.

Gibbons, Euell. *Stalking the Wild Asparagus*. New York: David McKay Co., Inc., 1970.

Godfrey, Bob, and Chelton, Dudley. *Climb: Rock Climbing in Colorado*. Boulder: Westview, 1977.

Hanrahan, James S., and Bushnell, David. *Space Biology: The Human Factor in Space Flight*. New York: Basic Books, 1960.

Healy, Trudy. *A Climber's Guide to the Adirondacks*. New York: Adirondack Mountain Club, 1972.

Herzog, Maurice. *Annapurna: The First Conquest of an Eight Thousand Meter Peak*. New York: E. P. Dutton & Co., 1953.

Huxley, Anthony. *Standard Encyclopedia of the World's Mountains*. New York: G. P. Putnam's Sons, 1962.

Jackson, Monica, and Stark, Elizabeth. *Tents in the Clouds: The First Women's Himalayan Expedition*. London: Collins, 1956.

James, Ron. *Rock Face: Techniques of Rock Climbing*. London: BBC Publications, 1974.

Jerome, John. *On Mountains*. New York: Harcourt Brace Jovanovich, Inc., 1978.

Kjellstrom, Bjorn. *Be Expert with Map and Compass: The Orienteering Handbook*, rev. ed. New York: Charles Scribner's Sons, 1976.

Lance, Kathryn. *Running for Health and Beauty: A Complete Guide for Women*. New York: Bobbs-Merrill Co., Inc., 1977.

Lederer, William J., and Wilson, Joe Pete. *Complete Cross-Country Skiing and Ski Touring*. New York: W. W. Norton & Co., Inc., 1972.

Lukan, Karl (ed.). *The Alps and Alpinism*. New York: Coward, McCann & Geoghegan, Inc., 1968.

Mead, Robert D. *Ultimate North: Canoeing Mackenzie's Arctic Great River*. New York: Doubleday & Co., Inc., 1976.

Miller, Irene, and Komarkova, Vera. "On the Summit." *National Geographic*, Vol. 155, #3, March 1979.

Milne, Malcolm (ed.). *The Book of Modern Mountaineering*. New York: G. P. Putnam's Sons, 1968.

Moses, Sam. *Stone Walls, Stout Hearts*. New York: Sports Illustrated Magazine, 1978.

Nesbitt, Paul H., Pond, Alonzo W., and Allen, William H. *The Survival Book*. New York: Funk & Wagnalls, Inc., 1959.

Newbery, Eric. *Great Ascents: A Narrative History of Mountaineering*. New York: Studio Books, The Viking Press, 1977.

Novak, Michael. *The Joy of Sports*. New York: Basic Books, 1976.

Pallister, Nancy (ed.). *NOLS Cookery*. Lawrence, Kansas: Teachers College Press, 1974.

Palmer, Bruce. *Body Weather*. New York: Jove Publications, Inc., 1976.

Petzoldt, Paul. *The Wilderness Handbook*. New York: W. W. Norton & Co., Inc., 1974.

Read, Piers Paul. *Alive*. New York: Avon Books, 1975.

Richards, Colette. *Climbing Blind*. New York: E. P. Dutton & Co., 1967.

Robbins, Royal. *Basic Rockcraft*. Glendale, Calif.: La Siesta Press, 1970.

Rosenfeld, Edward. *The Book of Highs*. New York: Quadrangle, 1973.

Roskolenko, Harry (ed.). *Solo: Great Adventures Alone*. New York: Playboy Press, 1973.

Rowell, Galen. "Climbing Half Dome the Hard Way." *National Geographic*, June 1974, p. 782.

Rudner, Ruth. *Wandering: A Walker's Guide to the Mountain Trails of Europe*. New York: The Dial Press, 1972.

Rutstrum, Calvin. *The Wilderness Route Finder*. New York: Macmillan, Inc., 1973.

Sheehan, George A. *Doctor Sheehan on Running*. New York: Bantam Books, Inc., 1978.

Snyder, Howard H. *The Hall of the Mountain King.* New York: Charles Scribner's Sons, 1975.

Spectorsky, Auguste C. (ed.). *The Book of the Mountains.* New York: Appleton-Century-Crofts, 1955.

Spencer, Sidney. *Mountaineering.* Seattle: The Mountaineers.

Stebbins, Ray. *Cold-Weather Camping.* Chicago: Henry Regnery Co., 1975.

Troebst, Cord C. *The Art of Survival.* New York: Doubleday & Co., Inc., 1975.

Ullyot, Joan. *Women's Running.* Mountain View, Calif.: World Publications, 1976.

Ward, Michael. *Mountain Medicine: A Clinical Study of Cold and High Altitudes.* New York: Beekman Publishers, Inc., 1975.

Weiss, Elizabeth. *Female Fatigue.* New York: Zebra Books, 1976.

Workman, Fanny Bullock, and Workman, William Hunter. *The Call of the Snowy Hispar.* London: Constable & Co., Ltd., 1910.

INDEX